ACTING EDITION

THE JOY RIDE

A Play in Three Acts

by

GEORGINA REID

Published by
**NEW PLAYWRIGHTS' NETWORK
35, SANDRINGHAM ROAD,
MACCLESFIELD,
CHESHIRE, SK10 1QB**

First Published September, 1972.
First Re-print October, 1974.
Second Re-print June, 1988.

ISBN 0 90365 312 5

PRODUCTION NOTES.

The set should be quite simple, even austere, and for the stage carpenter it has two great advantages. It needs neither doors nor window frames. A touch of comfort is supplied by a few rich hangings and possibly a sheepskin rug or two.

The costumes should be quite colourful but it would be wise to avoid shiny fabrics or anything too garish. Remember that Codiva and Leofric are rich and their clothing should appear to be of good quality. Both men's and women's costumes are easily made and hiring should be quite unnecessary. The head-dress so essential for hiding Godiva's hair in the second act can be made more attractive if a sort of simple tiara is worn on top of it.

Wigs are a problem but braids can sometimes be substituted. In either case, they *must* be long enough. A shoulder length wig would be ludricous for any one of the three young women.

The characters are fairly straightforward, but two of them have to change quite noticeably during the course of the play. Godiva has to change from a rather pathetic dumb blonde to someone more bitchy and overbearing in the second act, then finally back to her original character. Edgar has to appear prudish and austere most of the time, but virile and eager when the occasion arises.

Moll is at all times completely sincere. When forced to have a vision it should be apparent that her first attempt is false and laboured, but when the real vision comes over her she is completely carried away.

When I wrote this scene I did not envisage a darkened stage with flickering flames and droning of bombers. However, some companies have added these effects with apparent success, and their inclusion is entirely at the discretion of the producer.

Georgina Reid.

CHARACTERS
In order of Appearance

Leofric
Margery
Old Moll
Thomas
Godiva
Hilda
Christina
Edgar

The action takes place in an upstairs room in a Saxon castle,
shortly before the Norman invasion.

Act One. A Summer Morning

Act Two. Next Morning

Act Three. That Afternoon

THE JOY RIDE

ACT ONE

SCENE — *An upstairs room in a Saxon castle, shortly before the Norman conquest. There are tapestries on the walls and two or three narrow windows without glass in the right wall. The back half of the stage forms a sort of dais, about eight inches higher than the front. On the dais, right, is a long refectory table with a bench in front of it. On it stand a pitcher and two wine cups. There is another bench down left and there are two rather splendid carved chairs, with ornamental tapestry, centre and down right. There is a woven rush mat on the floor, curtained exits down left and down left and down right and an open archway in the back wall, left.*
Leofric, a nobleman of about forty, rather stout and ruddy, is staring moodily out of the rearmost window. MARGERY,
a servant girl, is sweeping the floor with a besom, down left.

LEOFRIC. *(angrily)* Rain! *(He turns, scowling)* Rain, Margery, Rain!

MARGERY. Yes, my lord.

LEO. *(Moving down and looking out of another window)* I thought of a hundred and one things that could go wrong today, but I never thought of rain, Margery, I never thought of rain.

MARGERY. No, my lord.

LEO. Nasty wet stuff, wherever you look. *(turns away from window)*

D'you think it's an omen, Margery?

MARGERY. An omen, my lord?

LEO. This day that I've planned for and hoped for and pinned
 my faith to . . . . . is it all a mistake, I wonder?

MARGERY. Old Moll don't make mistakes, sir. If Old Moll
 dreamed it, it must come true.

LEO. Yes, of course, it must come true. I know it will, only . . . .
 I wish it was all over. It's so new, so different from anything
 that's happened before. It'll be magnificent, Margery . . . . . If
 it only stops raining.
 (OLD MOLL *appears in archway at the back. She is dirty,
 unkempt, picturesque, and of advanced years. She laughs
 quietly and he turns.)*

LEO. Old Moll, tell me. In your vision, was it raining?

MOLL. In my vision the sun shone. The sky was cloudless blue.
 (MOLL *advances to centre front with a shuffling step.)*

LEO. Then, if it rains, she doesn't go?

MOLL. If it rains she still goes. No matter what, she still goes. It
 is her destiny.
 (Exit OLD MOLL, *down left)*

LEO. Of course, her destiny and mine. Poor little woman.

MARGERY. There's half an hour to go yet, sir. It may clear up,
 sudden like.

LEO. Huh! In half an hour the river Sherbourne will have burst
 its banks and the road will be impassable.

MARGERY. *(smiling)* Oh no, sir, indeed it won't.

LEO. *(suddenly angry)* Don't contradict me, girl. This is my
 great day that's going to be ruined!

MARGERY. *(not a bit frightened)* And her ladyship's, sir.

LEO. And her ladyship's, of course.

MARGERY. I hope her ladyship is feeling in good spirits.

LEO. In good spirits? She's never been in better spirits. She can't

wait for the great moment to arrive. She's excited, that's what
she is, excited.
(He exits, up left.)
MARGERY. *(dryly)* Very natural. So should I be in her place.
*(She goes on sweeping. After a moment THOMAS peers
round the door curtain, down left, and sneaks in, rather
furtively. He is a thin, nervous young fellow with a sudden
gay smile and sudden moments of sadness. He is dressed in a
decent red jerkin.)*
THOMAS. Oh, *you're* here, Margery.
MARGERY. Thomas! Have you lost your way? The kitchens are
down the back stairs.
THOMAS. I know it, my girl. I've just delivered two great heavy
baskets of bread down there.
MARGERY. Then what are you up here for? And why are you
wearing your best red tunic as if it was a Holy Day?
THOMAS. I want to see Earl Leofric.
MARGERY. Huh! It's not very likely he'll want to see *you*, a
common baker's boy, on such an important day as this.
Whatever made you choose today of all days?
THOMAS. It's now or never, that's what. It's taken me long
enough to get my courage up and now I've reached the
point when I daren't go back for fear I never come again. Tell
me, Margery, is he very terrible?
MARGERY. *(laughing)* Terrible? Lord bless you, that's just a
silly rumour. It pleases him to think that everyone's afraid of
him, so he makes a lot of noise and scowls and stamps and
roars, but he's really quite harmless.
THOMAS. *(not convinced)* Oh. Well, I'll wait here for a while.
(Sits on bench, down left.)
MARGERY. Until he comes back?
THOMAS. Or until I run away.

MARGERY. What? After coming here in your best red jerkin?
  Are you such a coward?
THOMAS. Oh, yes, Margery, I'm a terrible coward. D'you know,
  if I looked down from that window to the courtyard below
  I'd turn quite faint and giddy.
MARGERY. *(scornfully)* Well, you're not much of a man, are
  you? I should be ashamed to admit it if I were you. Mind
  your feet!
  (She sweeps vigorously round him. He watches her.)
THOMAS. *(after a pause)* Margery's mostly mild and biddable;
  Why is she suddenly so formidable?
MARGERY. *(pausing)* Eh?
THOMAS. What makes a maiden, small and pliant,
  Grow to a fearsome female giant?
  Give her a five foot broom to brandish
  And lo, she's filled with some outlandish
  Magic power that makes the dust
  Flee in a frightened little gust.
MARGERY. *(astonished)* When did you make that up?
THOMAS. It just came into my head when I was watching you.
MARGERY. Oh, I don't believe it. You're an awful liar, Thomas.
  It's something you learned off a strolling player.
  (She raises the edge of the mat and sweeps the dust under it.)
THOMAS. And while she scoffs at my harmless chatting
  She sweeps the dust back under the matting!
MARGERY. *(Laughing)* You wretch! I don't know how you can
  think so fast. Do one about Old Moll. Go, on!
THOMAS. *(rising)* Old Moll, the soothsayer? All right.
  *(He stands a moment, thinking, bent like an old crone. Then
  he extends a clawlike hand and grips her.)*
THOMAS. Come now, pretty dearie,
  What have you to fear?

Maybe Moll is eerie,
Maybe Moll is queer,
Wrinkled, thin and wiry,
Ragged in her dress,
Fierce her eye and fiery,
Wild her grimy tress.

Do'ee think she'll hurt'ee?
Come now, maiden, speak.
Say she's just a dirty
Troublesome old freak.
Say her power of sooth is
Just a lot of bosh
Say the simple truth is
That she needs a wash!

MARGERY. *(stifling a giggle)* Thomas, you mustn't. It isn't safe
to make fun of Old Moll. She'll put the evil eye on you.

THOMAS. You don't believe that, do you?

MARGERY. What I believe doesn't matter. What matters is that
Earl Leofric believes every word she utters. If once Old Moll
takes against you, you won't get far with the master.

THOMAS. Thanks for the advice. I'll remember that.
(He wanders across to the window and looks up at the sky.)

THOMAS. So our lord Leofric is superstitious, is he? That could
be useful.

MARGERY. What do you mean?

THOMAS. Maybe I could beat the old hag at her own game.
Where is she now?

MARGERY. I don't know. Wandering around having visions, I
shouldn't wonder.

THOMAS. Does she often have them?

MARGERY. Old Moll gets visions like some people get hiccups.

She dreamed up this stunt that's on today.

THOMAS. "Stunt", girl? You call this a stunt, this wonderful event? This living poetry that is to take place in our blessed town?

MARGERY.   Oh, you're as silly as his lordship about it. Look out, here he comes.

(She turns to go)

THOMAS. Margery, don't leave me!

(But MARGERY has gone, down left, and EARL LEOFRIC is standing in the archway at the back, looking displeased. THOMAS faces him in obvious fright, backing down right)

LEOFRIC. Who are you and what do you want?

THOMAS. Thomas is my name sir and I want a job in your household. Please.

LEO. You're mighty well dressed for a down and out.

THOMAS. I'm not a down and out, sir. I'm a baker's boy. I help my father in our shop overlooking the Grey Friars'.

LEO. But I wasn't aware that I needed any more kitchen staff.

(advancing to centre front)

THOMAS. No, my lord. I don't want that sort of job. I'll go *mad* if I have to bake any more bread.

LEO. Go mad, will you? I don't think I want to employ anyone on the verge of lunacy.

THOMAS. *(immediately hopeless)* No, sir.

(Pause)

LEO. Well, speak up man. What can you do?

THOMAS. I'm an . . . . . an entertainer.

LEO. *(turning away fretfully)* Oh, one of those singing lute players. I've got one already.

THOMAS. No sir, I don't sing. I *can't* sing. And I can't play the lute. I did try but it seems I've no ear for music.

LEO. *(surprised)* That makes a change, anyway. Everybody else I know seems to be obsessed with the stuff. It depresses me, as a matter of fact. My wife tells me I'm tone deaf.

THOMAS. Never mind, sir. "He who cannot sing a song shall save his breath and live more long".

LEO. *(pleased)* That's good. I've not heard that before. "He who cannot sing a song shall save his breath and live more long". I'll tell my wife that the next time she's admiring that long-haired lute player. Cedric, his name is. A big blonde brute with teeth like tombstones. You may have seen him.

THOMAS. No, my lord. I don't go out much, you see. I bake bread all night and sleep all day.

LEO. Well, why aren't you in bed now? Oh yes, you're looking for a job as an entertainer. But if you can't sing or play, what *can* you do? Are you a juggler?

THOMAS. No . . . . . Yes, in a way I am. I juggle with words. I'm a rhymer, my lord.

LEO. A rhymer, eh? A fellow who says funny things in rhyme?

THOMAS. They're not always funny, sir.

LEO. How can they be entertaining if they're not funny?

THOMAS. Doesn't Cedric the lute player ever sing sad songs?

LEO. Yes, but that's when I find him funny. Well, let's hear one of your sad rhymes. It'll be in keeping with the weather.
(He sits moodily in large chair, centre)

THOMAS. A sad rhyme? I was sad last night. I'll tell you about last night.
(As he speaks the lines of verse, without undue emphasis on the rhymes, he acts the story so as to make a little one man comedy.)
To the place of my employment, empty of the least enjoyment,
This unhappy baker's boy went, full of groans and sighs.
Fast the busy hours were speeding, all night long I worked unheeding,

Mixing, flouring, shaping, kneading, bread and cakes and pies.
'Neath my hands the restless dough seemed a living creature, so
I dealt it a tremendous blow, but that was most unwise.
Next in baking tins I laid it, on the oven shelves arrayed it,
And most fervently I prayed it would not fail to rise.
True it rose, there's no disguising, that would hardly be
surprising,
But I could not stop it rising, past all normal size!
Like balloons my loaves were growing; where they'd stop there
was no knowing,
Heaving, looming, overflowing, right before my eyes.
They had *faces*, brown and wily, crusty smiles that simpered
shyly,
Beady eyes that glittered slyly, bread in human guise!
And I heard soft voices sighing, "Look at us, we're really
trying.
Bread like us is bread worth buying. We deserve a prize".
Cold with fear I backed a pace, slammed the oven in their face,
Still their voices filled the place with distant doughy cries.
Oh, my lord, I'll not go back although you stretched me on
the rack,
And though the bread be all burned black, I will not watch it
rise!

LEO. So that's a sample of your sadness. Hmmm!

THOMAS. Were you . . . . entertained, my lord?

LEO. A little, a little. But it's childish stuff and I'm in no mood
for such trifles. *(rises)* My mind is on the big event of the day
and until that's over I'm in torment. Simply in torment.

THOMAS. I was wrong to intrude on you at such a time.

LEO. Maybe. Go away, young man, and return again tomorrow.

THOMAS. And will you tell me tomorrow if you'll take me on?

LEO. I'll decide that when you have rhymed me a description of this day of destiny.

THOMAS. *(staggered)* A description of this day? Of my lady?

LEO. Yes. If I like your verses I'll have them written down for her to keep.

THOMAS. But my lord, I'm not allowed to watch!

LEO. *(in sudden anger)* I know that, you fool. But you know what's going to happen and you have your imagination, haven't you?

THOMAS. Yes sir. I'll try, but . . . . .

LEO. *(crossing to right)* And don't omit to mention the weather. Oh, this cursed rain! *(shakes his fist at the sky)*

THOMAS. *(urgently)* Don't do that, sir!

LEO. Don't do what?

THOMAS. Don't raise your fist at the rain. It's unlucky.

LEO. Is it? I've never heard it said.

THOMAS. Never heard the old rhyme?

   If at Heaven you raise your fist, heavy showers will persist, But if you raise your face and smile the rain will cease in a little while.

LEO. That's interesting. Where'd you hear it?

THOMAS. My Granny, sir. She was known as The Wise Woman of Warwickshire. She knew a hundred such sayings and lived to a great old age.

LEO. You know all these sayings?

THOMAS. Most of them sir. She used to teach 'em to me instead of nursery rhymes.

LEO. Splendid. How did it go? "If you raise your face and smile . ."

THOMAS. "The rain will cease in a little while".

LEO. Very interesting. Nothing in it, of course, but I'm a keen student of folk lore. You must tell me some more some time. Now, off with you.

THOMAS. *(bowing)* Yes, my lord. Thank you, my lord.

(He goes out, down left. As soon as he is gone LEOFRIC *hurries to the window and smiles hopefully upwards. His smile should be visible to most of the audience. As he stands there,* GODIVA *enters at the back and stands woefully in the archway. She is young and pretty but rather shallow and discontented. Her long blonde hair is in two braids.)*

GODIVA. Any improvement?

LEO. *(turning, still smiling)* Not a sign, my dear.

GODIVA. Then what are you grinning about?

LEO. *(wiping off grin)* Grinning, my love? No, truly, there's nothing to grin about.

GODIVA. That's the truest word you've spoken today. My God, how I ever got mixed up in it I don't know. *(sits dejectedly in centre chair)* If I could back out of it I would. But it's too late. The town criers have made a public wonder of it from here to York. Oh, I wish I were dead!
(Her face crumples, like a child about to cry. LEOFRIC *hurries to her, kneels and puts his arms round her.)*

LEO. There, there, Leo's little love. Be brave. It'll soon be over and then you'll be a great heroine and I shall be famous.

GODIVA. I hope so. I'm only doing it for you, Leo. I hope you realise that.

LEO. And for the poor people. Remember them.

GODIVA. That's a lot of nonsense and you know it.

LEO. But Old Moll's vision . . . . .

GODIVA. If anyone mentions Old Moll's vision again, I shall scream! There's been a scream coming up inside me ever since she arrived and before long it'll break out! *(wildly)* It will, Leo! Any moment now, I won't be able to hold it back . . .

LEO. *(dashing to table for cup of wine, already poured)* No, no! You must get a grip on yourself. Here, drink this. It'll steady your nerves.

(She tosses it off and he pours her another which she holds and pouts over.)

GODIVA. And why does it have to be a *white* horse? You know I'm only happy on my little black pony.

LEO. If Old Moll saw a white horse, you'll have to ride a white horse.

GODIVA. But it isn't a bit smart. Blondes look better on black. *(She drinks)*

LEO. You'll look lovely on Buster. He's the best horse in my stable.

GODIVA. Buster, I ask you! And he's so enormous, I'll never be able to mount him.

LEO. Dearest, the mounting block is an excellent height.

GODIVA. It isn't that. You don't realise because you don't have to ride side saddle, but I never know which foot to put into the stirrup first. One of these days I shall ride down the street facing the back end of the horse! *(drinks)*

LEO. *(patiently)* Silly girl, you just get the horse's head on your *left* and put your *right* foot in the stirrup. It's perfectly simple, isn't it?

GODIVA. Yes, I suppose it is . . . . . if you can remember which is your right foot!

LEO. *(giving up)* Oh, never mind, love. Get Margery to help you mount.

GODIVA. I don't want Margery. She looks at me with contempt. All the servants do. None of them respect me as they should.

LEO. My dear, if you could be more commanding . . . .

GODIVA. I *am* commanding. I keep on commanding. Half the time they don't obey me.

Enter MOLL, down left. She advances to centre stage, folds her arms and looks down at GODIVA. She nods slowly.

MOLL. The hour will soon be nigh.

(Exit MOLL, *up left.)*

GODIVA. I'm going to scream! It's the effect she has on me. I
    shall, Leo, I shall!

LEO. *(rushing with pitcher to refill her cup)* I forbid you to
    scream. Here, have another drink.
    (She does so.)

GODIVA. Leo, hasn't it stopped raining?
    (He hastens to window and looks out.)

LEO. No dear, I'm afraid not.
    (He glances down and is startled.) By the beard of Rollo!
    Someone is coming to call!

GODIVA. Visitors?

LEO. *(furiously)* Visitors. Three of them, on horseback. Have
    they no sense, coming here on this day, at this hour?

GODIVA. What difference does it make? I wouldn't care if
    Canute himself came to call.

LEO. Maybe you wouldn't. But from what I can see, it's not
    Canute, it's your mother!

GODIVA. *(starting up, appalled)* My mother? Oh, dear God, I
    didn't think the outlook could be any blacker, but I was
    wrong.

LEO. D'you think she's heard?

GODIVA. Well, of *course* she's heard. You've had your wretched
    town criers out in every town and village for miles around.
    Did you imagine they'd miss out Lichfield? I could have told
    you this would happen.

LEO. *(with bravado)* Well, what if you could? We've no need to
    act like a pair of frightened children. She's only a woman.

GODIVA. I'm not so sure. I remember what my father called her.

LEO. What did he call her?

GODIVA. The wrath of God in female clothing.

LEO. Your father was a braver man than I am. *(crosses to left.)*

She'll try to stop us; you realise that, don't you?

GODIVA. *(miserably)* Yes. *(She sinks back into chair)*

LEO. We mustn't let her. We must be strong. Promise me you'll be strong.

GODIVA. I'll try, but . . . .

LEO. You must, dear. You know how much this means to me. *(He puts her cup and pitcher on table. They wait in silence, holding hands. After a moment, LADY HILDA enters by archway at the back. She is a domineering woman with a biting tongue.)*

HILDA. *(pausing dramatically in the archway)* Godiva! What does this mean?

GODIVA. *(rising nervously)* Mother, what a nice surprise! *(She kisses her half-heartedly.)*

HILDA. I am prepared to believe that it is a surprise.

LEO. *(giving her a careful embrace)* Why didn't you send a messenger?

HILDA. Because if I had, you would have made all speed to perform this little play before I arrived.

LEO. I don't know what you . . . . .

HILDA. Godiva! Is it true that you are going ride through the streets of Coventry, *stark naked?*

LEO. Oh, not *stark*, naked, mother. She has such a lot of hair.

HILDA. But no clothes?

LEO. Well, not exactly.

HILDA. Not a stitch?

LEO. Er . . . . . .no.

HILDA. Then I repeat, *stark naked.* Godiva, what have you to say?

GODIVA. *(sitting down, ready to weep)* I'm doing it to please LEO.

HILDA. To please Leo? *(turning to him in amazement)* The

noble lord Leofric, Earl of Chester and Lord of Coventry, is *pleased* to send his wife out on the streets in a state of utter nudity?

LEO. But her hair will hide . . . .

HILDA. Her hair will hide nothing. There is a strong wind blowing.

LEO. Nevertheless, she must go. If you'd just let me explain . . .

HILDA. *(seating herself heavily, down right)* Leofric, I am aghast. When you married my daughter I thought you a foolish man, but well-meaning and rich enough to keep Godiva happy. Now I realise that harmless exterior hides an evil undreamed of. My child, I have married you to a monster.

GODIVA. Oh no, mother, honestly, Leo isn't like that.

HILDA. Do you suggest there is some simple explanation for this scandalous project? The only alternative that I can see is lunacy. I often had my doubts about Leo's father . . .

LEO. Mother, I can explain everything.

HILDA. Then do so. No, don't.First we must wait for Godiva's sister and her husband. They are seeing to the horses.

GODIVA. *(rising)* Christina is with you? And Edgar?

HILDA. Naturally. You wouldn't expect me to ride from Lichfield alone?

GODIVA. Oh, whatever will Edgar say!

HILDA. Edgar is practically speechless.

LEO. Well, that's a relief from his usual preaching.

HILDA. Enough of that, Leofric. Your brother-in-law is a good, devout man and moreover, *he* has never sent his wife through the streets stark naked!

LEO. Well, there's still time. I'll lend him Old Moll and see what happens.

HILDA. May I be informed what this elderly female named Moll has to do with it?

GODIVA. She has everything to do with it. If it hadn't been for
  her . . . .

HILDA. Say no more! I hear Christina's foot on the stair. She
  too will want to hear her sister's explanation of this
  incredible affair.

  *(Enter CHRISTINA, centre back. She is a lovely girl of
  seventeen with long dark hair in braids. Her eyes are full of
  eagerness and vitality which she is at pains to hide under an
  appearance of demure restraint when her husband EDGAR is
  present. He follows her into the room, a tall thin, ascetic-
  looking man with longish hair and a forked beard. He has a
  serious way of speaking and an attractive, if saintly smile.)*

CHRISTINA. *(going first to GODIVA and kissing her)* Godiva!
  It's not true, is it?

  (GODIVA looks helpless. LEO intervenes.)

LEO. Little Christina! How lovely to see you.

CHRISTINA. My lord Leofric. *(curtseys)* I hope you are well.

LEO. Splendid. Never felt better. And don't you look a picture,
  eh? *(turns to EDGAR)* Married life agrees with her, eh Edgar?

EDGAR. *(with a grave smile)* It is indeed a felicitious state for
  both of us.

LEO. By the Beard of Rollo! I can't believe it was only a month
  ago we came to your wedding. What a day, eh, Christina?
  Shall I ever forget it? That wine really went to my head. Got
  any of it left, Edgar, or have you scoffed the lot?

EDGAR. No, we've been very temperate in our drinking, have we
  not, my dear?

CHRISTINA. Oh, very. You see, wine inflames the senses.
  *(Her eyes are cast down but her mouth is mutinous. She
  crosses and sits on bench, down left.)*

LEO. *(taken aback)* Oh yes, so it does. Godiva, we had better
  serve something a little milder at dinner.

GODIVA. *(bitterly)* At dinner? You expect me to think of dinner
at a time like this?

HILDA. That is just one more proof that your husband is a
heartless wretch. Edgar, if you are a true man, reason with this
villain and bring him to his senses.

EDGAR. Leofric, I cannot believe that you intend to defile and
humiliate a woman as pure and good as your wife, a woman
whose virtue and honour are renowned throughout the land . . .

LEO. You've got it all wrong. Nobody's going to defile my wife.

EDGAR. Oh my brother, any man who would expose his wife's
naked flesh to the lustful gaze of the common multitude . . . .

LEO. *(angrily)* I'm not exposing her to anything of the sort.
There's not a man or woman in the street, by my order. Every
window and door is shuttered and barred and nobody dares
to look out for fear of being thrown into prison for life.

HILDA. *(thumping the arm of her chair)* But that's not the point.
Whether she is seen or not seen, why is she doing it? Why?

LEO. Well, I was going to explain but . . . .

HILDA. I wish to hear the answer from my own daughter and
from nobody else.
(LEO *fumes silently and goes and peers out of window.)*

HILDA. Well, Godiva, answer me.

GODIVA. *(almost in a whisper)* Its . . . . to save the poor people.

HILDA. The poor people? What poor people?

GODIVA. The people of Coventry.

HILDA. From what are they to be saved?

GODIVA. From paying more taxes.

HILDA. In heaven's name, why shouldn't they pay more taxes?

GODIVA. They pay so many already.

HILDA. It's odd that it never worried you before. All your life,
whenever you needed new clothes, fine horses, extra rooms
added to the castle, your father always raised the money by

taxing the people. Now it's your husband's place to do the same. Why make a fuss about it?

GODIVA. I didn't . I only mentioned it.

CHRIS. I don't see what taxes have to do with it.

HILDA. Neither do I. The misery of the poor is totally irrelevant. Or had you hoped to take their minds off their troubles by a display of nudity?

GODIVA. Mother, please! If you'd try to understand.

HILDA. I am trying most anxiously, I do assure you. It's no small matter when the wife of an earl and the niece of a bishop seeks to drag her family name in the dust.

LEO. In the mud more likely.

(He tries one more attempt at smiling up at the rain. HILDA turns and observes this with surprise.)

EDGAR. *(approaching GODIVA)* Think of the bishop, dear Godiva. That frail and pious old man. Consider what this reckless exhibition will do to him, your own uncle.

HILDA. Your own husband seems to consider it with great glee!
(LEO hastily sobers up.)

EDGAR. Dear Lady Godiva, have you spoken to your priest about this? Has he given his consent?

GODIVA. Father Benedict says I may go if I take six nuns with me, to walk on either side of my horse.

EDGAR. And he has given his consent? I can hardly believe it.

GODIVA. He didn't at first but Leo threatened him.

LEO. *(exploding)* I did nothing of the sort! I. . . . I talked to him and then I gave him a pair of gold candlesticks.

HILDA. Sin upon sin! You bribed him! Are we never to get to the bottom of this tale of iniquity?

CHRIS. Mother dear, we might if you'd be quiet and let Godiva explain.

HILDA. I've given her every chance and all she does is gibber some nonsense which is no explanation at all. Will some kind person give me the real reason why my daughter is bent on indecent exposure?

(During this speech OLD MOLL *appears in archway at back and listens.)*

MOLL. She has no choice. It is her destiny.

HILDA. *(after amomentary silence)*
Who is this . . . . . creature?

GODIVA. It's Old Moll. She's the cause of everything. She had a vision.

LEO. Come in, Moll. I'm glad you've come. You'll be able to explain to my mother-in-law about your vision.

*(*OLD MOLL *comes down centre, helping herself to an apple from bowl on table as she passes.)*

MOLL. I'm sick of telling people about my vision. Tell her yourself.

HILDA. Woman, you forget youself! Leo, have her thrown out this instant.

*(*MOLL *sits on edge of dais, centre, her dirty cloak wrapped around her knees and enjoys her apple noisily.)* Godiva, aren't you going to send this wretched creature to the servants' quarters?

GODIVA. I daren't, mother.

HILDA. Daren't? Are you not mistress in this place? She's filthy! What is she doing in your household?

GODIVA. She just walked in one day, a few weeks ago. She does just what she likes and everyone is afraid of her.

*(*OLD MOLL *spits out a pip, noisily)*

HILDA. Well, I'm not afraid of her and if you think I'm going to have her spitting at me . . . .

LEO. *(intervening)* Mother, I beg you, be calm. Be polite. Old Moll is a soothsayer.

CHRIS. A soothsayer? Do you mean she can foretell the future?

HILDA. *(interested)* A soothsayer indeed? I believe they are all the rage at court this year.

CHRIS. There now, Godiva, your Old Moll is the height of fashion.

HILDA. If anything so dirty *can* be fashionable.

MOLL. I don't like the old one.

HILDA. *(indignantly)* Old one! You. . . . .

LEO. *(quickly)* Moll, if she could hear about your vision she wouldn't scoff any more. Won't you tell it again. No-one can tell it like you.

MOLL. Can I have another apple?

LEO. Of course, of course. Take the biggest. *(He passes her the bowl. She examines them slowly before selecting one)*

MOLL. *(addressing no-one in particular, looking at the apple and scratching herself)* I was fasting at the time. I only get visions on an empty stomach. It was the time of the full moon and I was sitting under a haystack.

HILDA. Drunk, I'll warrant.

MOLL. *(calmly)* I was not drunk and I was not dreaming. As I sat there My Lady Godiva appeared before me. She had on a dark red dress with fur round the hem and her hair was braided with gold. I had never seen her in my life but I knew who she was. "Moll," she said, "The people are unhappy. They are hungry and over-taxed. I see their sad faces wherever I go and hear them crying out for help. What ought I to do?" "Go to your lord," I said, "Tell him that if he eases the people's burden, you will do whatever he asks." After I said that, the vision faded and I got up. *(She bites and chews reflectively)*

EDGAR. I can't see how that vision ties up with this other affair.

MOLL. That young man can't see yet, but he may soon. After I'd stumbled along in the dark I fell into a ditch.

HILDA. I *said* she was drunk.

MOLL. The old bitch has got drink on the brain. It was
    comfortable in the ditch and dry and fairly warm. I lay there
    for a bit, looking up at the stars, and I heard a man's voice
    saying as if from up in the sky, "Godiva! Godiva! If you
    want to save the people, you must ride through Coventry with
    nothing to clothe you but your hair." Then he said it again.
    "Nothing but your hair". It was *him (jerks thumb at* LEO*)* He
    always says things twice.
LEO. That's quite true. It's a habit of mine.
MOLL. Then the other vision appeared. It was Godiva again, and
    she was sitting naked on a white horse. She looked very
    pretty. The sun was shining and I could hear the horse's
    hooves going clop-clop on the cobbles. Then that vision faded
    too, so in the morning I got a lift into Coventry and came and
    told his Lordship. He was very pleased.
HILDA. *(staggered)* Pleased!
LEO. *(defensively)* Yes, pleased. I'd had a few pricks of conscience
    about the poor folks and I'd been wondering how to ease
    their taxes without losing face. You know, they think of me
    as a stern military type of man and I didn't want to destroy
    that image of me by doing something soft. This vision provided
    me with a good way out.
EDGAR. You can call it "good", Leofric?
LEO. Dash it, Edgar, there's nothing lewd in *my* mind when I
    picture the scene. I find it . . . . . well . . . rather charming. And
    it's going to make Coventry famous.
HILDA. Infamous, you mean. It'll do that all right. And all because
    this senile, maundering old fool dreams up a pack of lies.
MOLL. *(rising and going to her)* Be careful what you say, Lady
    Hilda. You weren't always such a virtuous person and neither
    was your brother the bishop.
HILDA. *(not quite so self-possessed)* What do you know about

me and the bishop?

MOLL. I know that when you and he were children you broke
into Lichfield cathedral and defaced a number of holy
pictures.

HILDA. It was a childish prank. That's all.

MOLL. There was a great outcry about it and some innocent man
was accused and publicly whipped. But you and your brother
said nothing.

HILDA. We were very young. Children don't realise. I've done
great penance in private.

CHRIS. Mother, we're not judging you . . . but how did Old Moll
know?

HILDA. Someone told her of course. The story must have
leaked out, though *I* never told a soul.

MOLL. You think someone told me? Then what about this?
When you were leaving Lichfield this morning, a dog ran in
front of your horse and it reared up and nearly threw you off.
An old man ran out of a cottage nearby and held its bridle. He
had a scar down his left cheek. You son-in-law gave him a
penny for his pains.

CHRIS. It's true, mother, every word of it is true! How
wonderful, she really *has* got second sight!

MOLL. *(going off, down left)* Drunk, indeed. That one needed to
be taught a lesson. But I showed her. Old Moll showed her.
(Exit, L.)

HILDA. *(rising)* I should like to go and lie down. I feel tired
after the journey.

GODIVA. You can have your usual room in the west turret.

HILDA. Thank you, Godiva. It seems that nothing I can say
will prevent this event from taking place, so let nobody come
near me until it is all over. I may rest but I don't suppose I
shall sleep. I'm far too disturbed.

(She sweeps out, with a glare, down right. Enter MARGERY
at the back.)

MARGERY. My lord, Sister Agnes has arrived with her nuns. And
   I think the rain is easing off.

LEO. *(rushing to the window)* Is it really? Yes, I see blue sky
   coming up rapidly. How marvellous! That rhyming fellow
   knew a thing or two. Now Margery, 1 want you to go and see
   that rooms are prepared for our three guests. *(Exit*
   MARGERY *at back)* Godiva, my love, I'll leave you now and
   take Edgar and Christina down to the kitchen for a bite to eat.
   They must be hungry after that ride . . . .

GODIVA. Not Christina! Stay with me, Christina!

CHRIS. Of course dear.

LEO. *(kissing* GODIVA*)* Don't keep Sister Agnes waiting, my love.
   The sun is starting to shine, you see? It's going to be all right.
   I shall be thinking of you all the time you're gone. All the
   time.

GODIVA. *(gripping him desperately)* Leo!

LEO. *(detatching her firmly)* Be brave, dearest. The sooner you
   start, the sooner it'll all be over, eh? Goodbye for now. Come
   along, Edgar.
   *(*LEO *and* EDGAR *exit, left.* GODIVA *fills her wine cup at
   table and sits forlornly, centre.)*

GODIVA. Have a drink, Christina?

CHRIS. No thanks, I've got out of the habit.

GODIVA. I don't usually drink much. It's just to give me courage.

CHRIS. *(going to window)* There are six nuns. I can't see their
   faces because of their hoods. How far will they have to walk?

GODIVA. I don't know. About five miles. *(drinks)*

CHRIS. I hope they're *young* nuns with good strong feet. What
   an odd life they lead. I pity them.

GODIVA. I envy them. They're not at the mercy of a husband's whims and fancies.

CHRIS. No. Maybe in their hearts they wish they were.
It must be fun being married to Leo.

GODIVA. Fun!

CHRIS. *(her face alive with excitement)* Yes, I think he's a sport,
arranging this affair for you. It's a pity you don't appreciate it.

GODIVA. Appreciate it? Don't you think it's awful?

CHRIS. No, I think it's gorgeous. Think of it! The empty streets,
the shuttered windows, the six grey nuns walking in pious
silence . . . . and you on your white horse, triumphant in
your naked beauty. I wish it were me. How I'd love to throw
off these stuffy constricting clothes and feel the free winds of
heaven on every part of my body. I wouldn't look down in
modesty: I'd throw back my head and laugh!

GODIVA. Christina! You're shocking!

CHRIS. Oh I suppose I am, to anyone brought up under the wing
of Uncle Steven. Don't tell anyone what I just said, though.
It might get back to Edgar.

GODIVA. I'm not surprised that you keep such thoughts from
Edgar. He's so devout, it's lovely to listen to him. *(drinks)*

CHRIS. Is it? I thought so once, too. Now I think perhaps *you*
should have married him and I should have had Leofric.

GODIVA. Christina! What are you saying?

CHRIS. Oh nothing. I didn't mean it. Only that I wish Old Moll
had seen me in her vision instead of you. But of course, if she
had, Edgar would have scotched the whole glorious idea. He'd
never let *his* wife have such fun.

GODIVA. *(rising and going to her)* Christina, the way you talk
about Edgar. And you've only been married a month.

CHRIS. A month? It feels like a year!

GODIVA. Something's wrong, isn't it? Don't you love him any
more?

CHRIS. *(crossing to left)* Love him? I adore him. I always have, ever since I first saw him. He's only got to touch me and I tremble all over, I love him so passionately.

GODIVA. Well then?

CHRIS. He doesn't want that sort of love. I asked him once what he most admired in a woman, and he answered that he liked women who were sweet and modest and gentle and chaste, just like me. Those were his very words, Godiva. "Just like you". Was anything so far from the truth? Oh, I *am* chaste, of course. One couldn't help it, living with the Bishop of Lichfield, but obviously he thinks I'm pure unsullied womanhood, complete with a dove in one hand and a lily in the other. And because I adore him, I have to live up to it. I'm getting very good at it, Godiva, have you noticed? I'm insufferably modest and unyieldingly chaste, but the effort is killing me.

GODIVA. Do you mean? . . . . . .

CHRIS. You know perfectly well what I mean, Godiva. When he looks at me, my legs turn to water.

GODIVA. *(crossing carefully to chair centre)* It's a funny thing about legs. *(sits)*

CHRIS. Uncle Steven said he's never known a man of such fine sensibility, such delicacy of feeling. He said, such a man placed women on a pedestal. He said, "Don't ever disillusion him or you'll break his heart".

GODIVA. But I don't understand. Doesn't he love you?

CHRIS. Of course he loves me. Only it's a sort of spiritual love. The love one might feel for an adored younger sister. *(crosses to right)*

GODIVA. Do you mean to say that all this month you've been married, he's never . . . . . .

CHRIS. *(looking out of window and abruptly changing subject)*

They're bringing out your horse, Godiva! And look, the sun is shining!

GODIVA. *(bleakly)* So it is. My last hope gone.

CHRIS. Your last hope?

GODIVA. If we could have had a really heavy storm with thunder and lightening Leo might have taken it as a sign not to go. *(drinks deeply)*

CHRIS. Poor Godiva. You're forcing yourself to do this, just to please Leo, aren't you?

GODIVA. *(speaking rather carefully, sometimes having trouble)* Yes. He's terribly kind and good to me, but I'm afraid I'm a terrible disappointment to him. The servants all despise me. His friends all ignore me because I don't joke and laugh with them. *(drinks)* I'm not clever at sports or music. There's nothing in me he can be proud of. I'm so afraid he'll stop loving me if I don't do this.

CHRIS. I can't for the life of me see why he doesn't just proclaim a repeal of the taxes if they're a weight on his conscience. There's no need for all this romantic pageant.

GODIVA. You don't understand Leo. He's always had a deep desire to be famous in some way, even after his death. He started off by being harsh and warlike, and made quite a name for himself, but he can't keep it up. It's not his real nature.

CHRIS. So he's making another bid for fame, by proxy as it were. It's rather clever in a way. He gets the taxes repealed and yet keeps his reputation as a stern and cruel man.

GODIVA. *(smiling a bit)* Christina, what can I say to Uncle Steven? He'll be livid.

CHRIS. Tell him no price was too high to pay for such a deed of charity. Honestly Godiva, the craziest things are done in the name of charity. You don't need to. . . . . .
(A bell starts to toll.)

CHRIS. What's that bell for?

GODIVA. *(blandly)* It's for me. It's the sign, to clear the streets because I'm coming. ·

(She drains her wine cup. MARGERY enters at the back and stands in the archway.)

MARGERY. It's time, my lady.

(GODIVA. sits still, smiling.)

CHRIS. It's time to get ready, Godiva.

GODIVA. Don't fuss, Christina. *(her speech is giving her trouble now)* They can't start the party without me.

(She stands up with difficulty, clinging to back of chair)

(giggling) It's going to be a hen party, so I don't suppose I shall enjoy it much. And I'll tell you another reason why I don't want to go to this party. I haven't a *thing* to wear!

(She slides slowly to her knees, still smiling happily. CHRIS and MARGERY stand appalled as the CURTAIN FALLS)

CURTAIN.

ACT TWO

The same. Next morning. LEO, HILDA, CHRISTINA *and*
EDGAR *are seated, having breakfast.* MARGERY *is serving them.*
There is cold meat, bread and ale on the table, four metal plates
and four tankards.
They are seated thus:-

HILDA   EDGAR

LEO

CHRISTINA

LEO. More venison, mother?

HILDA. No thank you, Leo.

LEO. Edgar? Christina? Oh, come, you've hardly eaten a thing.

CHRIS. I've had as much as you, Leo. What's happened to your
usual appetite?

LEO. Oh, I'm too excited to eat. It's not every morning you wake
up and find yourself famous. Come, let's drink a toast. To
Godiva, the heroine of Coventry!

CHRIS. To Godiva! *(She and* LEO *drink)*

LEO. Edgar, you don't drink to my wife?

EDGAR. *(peaceably)* My cup is empty, Leofric. But I join with
you in admiration of your wife.

CHRIS. I thought you disapproved, Edgar.

EDGAR. So I do, most heartily. What she did was a thing no
modest, well-bred woman should do. But I cannot help
admiring her courage.

HILDA. Neither can I. It's the most remarkable thing. As a child
she was the most timid creature alive. Quite frankly, I wouldn't
have believed her capable.

LEO. *(beaming)* There now, mother. Your timid daughter has
surprised you and you like it.

HILDA. For Godiva I have nothing but admiration. For the man
who caused her to do it, I cannot conceal my displeasure.

LEO. Oh, nonsense, mother. Look what good will come of it.
The poor people are delighted. I've had a horde of them
outside the back door since sunrise, crying out their thanks
and calling down blessing on my name. Isn't that a good
thing? Isn't it, Edgar? Wouldn't you let *your* wife do a kind
act to ease the burden of the poor?

EDGAR. Of course, if I . . ..

LEO. Of course you would, and very pretty she'd look, riding
round Lichfield in her birthday suit. Why, come to think of it .

EDGAR. *(rising in sudden fury)* God damn you, Leo! I won't
have my wife's name connected with your vile schemes. You
shan't soil her with your filthy thoughts!

LEO. I only said . . . .

EDGAR. Shut up! Your beastliness is making her blush. Just you
keep your lewd imagination off her. My wife's virtue is not a
subject for coarse jokes at the breakfast table.
*(He crosses down left, scowling. Christina rises in distress and
goes to him.)*

CHRIS. Edgar, please! Leo meant no harm. Please, we are guests
in his house.

EDGAR. My love, you're too young and innocent to know the
vileness of men's thoughts. I value your innocence and I'll
fight any man to preserve it.

CHRIS. *(turning away, right, with a sigh)* My innocence is in no
danger from anyone here.

EDGAR. I hope not. I think I'd better take a turn on the
ramparts, to cool my temper.
CHRIS. Shall I come with you, dear?
EDGAR. No thanks, I should be rotten company in my present
mood. You stay and make my apologies to your brother-in-law.
(Exit right)
CHRIS. *(to* LEO, *who has risen)* Leo, I'm so sorry. I've never
heard him so angry and rude.
LEO. Think nothing of it, dear child. It was my fault, I suppose,
but I'd no idea he was so touchy.
CHRIS. *(sadly)* Edgar believes in keeping women on a pedestal.
HILDA. Edgar is a man in a thousand. My heart swells with
gratitude that God has sent a virtuous husband to *one* of my
daughters.
CHRIS. *(sitting on bench, down left)* Now, mother, you must
stop getting at Leo. He's the most well-meaning of men and
Godiva dotes on him.
LEO. *(delighted)* Does, she, the darling? I wish she'd come down.
I want to tell her what a fine brave girl she is.
CHRIS. Haven't you told her yet?
LEO. I've not clapped eyes on her since yesterday morning!
Soon as she got back from her ride she locked herself in her
room and wouldn't speak to anyone.
HILDA. Has she had anything to eat?
LEO. Yes, Margery took her some food and drink last night and
again this morning. She wouldn't let anyone else in.
CHRIS. How did she seem, Margery?
(MARGERY, *who has been standing quietly against the wall
comes forward.)*
MARGERY. She seemed upset last night and wouldn't talk. She
looked as if she'd been weeping.
LEO. Poor child.

MARGERY. But this morning she looked a great deal better. She
    asked what all the bells were ringing for. "For you, my lady,"
    I said, "You're a real heroine". Then we stood at the window
    and heard the people shouting "Long Live Godiva!" and she
    took a long breath and held up her head and said "Now Leo
    will be proud of me."

LEO. *(emotionally)* The sweet thing. No man could be prouder.
    (He turns away, right. After a pause HILDA *rises and comes
    down right)*

HILDA. *(acidly)* While his lordship masters his emotion, you'd
    better clear the table, Margery. We may be receiving callers.

MARGERY. Yes, my lady. They've already started. *(She begins
    to pile plates and tankards on a large tray.)*

HILDA. *(turning in surprise)* What do you mean? Who has called?

MARGERY. There's a protest committee from the League of
    Decency: six women, waiting downstairs to see his lordship.

HILDA. The League of Decency? I never heard of it.

LEO. *(turning)* A protest committee? I hadn't expected that.
    D'you think I should . . . . . ?

HILDA. *(sitting down right)* No. Let them wait. I've no patience
    with these women. They should stay at home and look
    after their families, not band together questioning the morals
    of their betters. I'll wager they're all as ugly as sin, eh?
    *(*MARGERY *pauses on her way to exit, left, with loaded tray)*

MARGERY. They do seem a plain lot, madam.

HILDA. Yes. The sort that have decency thrust upon them, and
    spend their lives making a virtue of
    (Exit MARGERY *left)*

LEO. Mother, I do believe you're on my side after all.

HILDA. Please understand that I'm not condoning your actions,
    Leofric. But I don't want Godiva upset by these people.
    (Enter GODIVA, *centre back)*

She deserves nothing but praise in her hour of triumph.

GODIVA. *(coming down right, smiling)* Mother, you're not angry with me any more.

(She is dressed in her best crimson dress with fur trimming. Important - Her hair is completely hidden by her headdress.)

HILDA. *(embracing her, still seated)* Of course not, dear. I'm very proud of you.

GODIVA. *(turning to LEO)* And you, Leo?

LEO. You were wonderful, my darling wonderful. *(kisses her)* I'm the proudest man in England.

(GODIVA gives a deep sigh of contentment and sinks into chair, centre. She now begins to look more regal and self-assured. MARGERY returns, down left, with empty tray, goes up to table and collects bread, meat etc.)

GODIVA. As I was coming across the courtyard just now, I was waylaid by the alchemist.

CHRIS. What on earth did *he* want?

GODIVA. He's manufacturing a new hair tonic and wants to know if he may call it "Godiva" Hair Tonic. He wants to claim that I owe my long, thick tresses to the regular use of his preparation.

LEO. He's got a nerve!

GODIVA. Nevertheless, I have said that he may, on condition that he provides us both with free medicines for the rest of his life. Was that a good idea, Leo?

LEO. Perfectly splendid, my love.

GODIVA. I thought you'd like it. You spend a small fortune on cough cures and liniments every winter. Margery, there are still a handful of people standing under my window. Please see that they all have half a cup of ale and then request them to go. Tell them, "Godiva sends her blessings to the good people of Coventry. Their gratitude makes my suffering worth while."

(MARGERY curtseys and exits, down left, with loaded tray.)
CHRIS. *(playfully)* Did you really suffer, Godiva?
HILDA. Naturally she suffered. Any gently reared woman would suffer agonies of shame and humiliation. Isn't that so, Godiva?
GODIVA. It was like that at first, Mother . . . . . . fetch me my footstool, Leo . . . . .but after my first feelings of shame had begun to abate, I found I could see the romantic side of it.
(LEO places footstool at her feet and then stands behind her)
HILDA. Romantic?
GODIVA. Yes. Can't you picture it? The empty streets, the shuttered windows, the six silent nuns, and me on my white horse, triumphant in my nakedness. Oh mother, for the first time in my life I felt the free winds of heaven on every part of my body.
HILDA. Good gracious me!
(CHRISTINA stares unbelievingly at GODIVA. She gives a rueful smile at hearing her own words repeated. MARGERY enters, down left and makes to cross room but checks on being spoken to.)
GODIVA. Margery!
MARGERY. Yes, my lady?
GODIVA. That venison you brought me for breakfast was rather high.
MARGERY. High, my lady?
GODIVA. Distinctly over-ripe. Could you not smell it?
MARGERY. I . . . . . I have a cold, my lady.
GODIVA. A poor excuse. It's come to something when an earl's lady is offered meat that's unfit for human consumption. *(rises)* I've a good mind to inspect the kitchens and see what goes on. Yes, I fancy a surprise visit will shake those scullions up a bit. Will you come, mother?
HILDA. *(rising)* With pleasure. And while we're there, let's clean

up Old Moll as well.

GODIVA. Oh no, hands off Old Moll. I wouldn't offend her for the world.

HILDA. Perhaps you're right. She might retaliate by having a vision of me, dancing round the graveyard in my night shift. The dear bishop would never survive the shock. Come along, Christina. Other women's kitchens are always more interesting than one's own.

(Exit GODIVA and HILDA, down left. CHRISTINA gives LEO a look of resignation and follows them out.) MARGERY wipes table with a cloth.)

LEO. *Was* that venison high, Margery?

MARGERY. I don't think so, my lord. It was from the same joint as you were eating yourself.

LEO. I can't say I tasted anything. But her ladyship has a more sensitive palate, I expect.

MARGERY. She seems in wonderful spirits this morning, sir.

LEO. Wonderful. Like a new woman, eh?

MARGERY. Yes, my lord.

(They smile at each other. EDGAR enters, right. MARGERY exits, left.)

EDGAR. *(awkwardly)* Leo . . . . . . I . . . .

LEO. *(turning)* Oh, Edgar, it's you. I'm glad you've come back, my dear chap. I wanted to apologise.

EDGAR. No no. It's I who should apologise. It was ridiculous of me to make such a fuss over a mere joke.

LEO. Yes, yes, of course, I was only joking. But I should have realised, to a man of you delicate feelings . . . . *(EDGAR turns away with a groan)* it must have been most upsetting. A fellow as gross as I am isn't used to such nobility of character.

EDGAR. To hell with my nobility of character!

LEO. Eh?

EDGAR. I said, to hell with my nobility of character.

LEO. *(gaping)* But . . . . you can't say that.

EDGAR. Oh yes I can and more besides. I can say I'm a sham and a hypocrite, with no more delicate feelings than a drunken pedlar. I can say blessings on Old Moll for dreaming up such a glorious vision. I can say, well done Godiva, and I wish I'd seen you riding by. I can say anything as long as *they're* not listening. *(sinks on bench, left.)*

LEO. They? Do you mean . . . . . .?

EDGAR. My wife and her mother. Leofric, I'm like a prisoner between two warders.

LEO. Oh, come now. Hilda's a bit fierce, I know, but Christina's a charming thing.

EDGAR. She's the worst, with her sweet innocent face and great trusting eyes. Do you realise, Leofric, that in her eyes I'm a plaster saint, all chastity, virtue and spiritual love?

LEO. And . . . .aren't you?

EDGAR. *(with a look)* No.

LEO. How did they get the wrong idea?

EDGAR. Oh, it was all the bishop's fault.

LEO. Uncle Stephen?

EDGAR. Yes, dear old Uncle Stephen. He may have defaced pictures in his far-off youth, but he's redeemed himself since then. Otherworldliness you'd never believe. He's always seen me through a sort of halo, ever since I was a choirboy with a treble voice and an angelic face. He wanted me to be a monk at one time; said I had a clear vocation. Naturally I hadn't the courage to tell him how far from the truth he was, and by that time I was in love with his niece, so if pure-souled, unstained manhood was what he was after, I went out to achieve it.

LEO. But, I never went to such lengths to get Godiva.

EDGAR. It's different when you're an earl with land and money. Besides, her father was alive when you married Godiva. She wasn't enclosed in her uncle's ecclesiastical grip.

LEO. Well, he accepted you, didn't he?

EDGAR. I gave him no peace for six months. But he wasn't keen on letting her marry *anyone*, you see. And in a way, he was right. She's not cut out for marriage. So gentle and modest and chaste . . . . . oh heaven, it ought not to be allowed!

LEO. What ought not to be allowed?

EDGAR. Girls like that.

LEO. Like what?

EDGAR. So beautiful. And so innocent. She's barely seventeen, Leo. Think of that! No more than a child. I'd be a brute to lay a finger on her.

LEO. You can't mean . . . .

EDGAR. Her uncle was right. She's too good for this world, he said. She thinks all men noble. "Never dis-illusion her," he said, "Or you'll break her heart." Oh Leo, much as I adore her, I'd give a lot if she were more like Godiva. You know, the sort of woman who could cast modesty to the winds in a good cause. Christina could no more do that wonderful ride than she could fly.

LEO. When I joked about it and you flew into a rage, were you shamming then?

EDGAR. *(getting up)* I was not. I was furious with you. Don't you see, *I* may be false as the devil, but *she isn't.* So for heaven's sake, keep a curb on your tongue when she's about or I'll knock your teeth in!

LEO. That's the spirit, lad. It does my heart good to find there's red blood in your veins after all.
(Enter THOMAS, *down left.)*
We'll have some sport together, now you're here. We'll get rid

of the women and . . . hello, who's this? Oh, yes, that young
rhyming fellow. What's your name again?

THOMAS. Thomas, my lord.

LEO. *(to EDGAR)* Thomas hopes to join my household, you
see. He's a rhymer and I've set him to make up a poem about
Godiva's ride. Have you done it, lad?

THOMAS. Yes, sir.

LEO. A long one, eh?

THOMAS. Not very long, sir. I had only my imagination and . . . .

LEO. Don't tell me that it let you down?

THOMAS. Never, my lord. But it tends to lead me astray.

LEO. *(laughing)* Lead you astray? Better get some girls to do that
for you.

THOMAS. Oh, I've had girls in plenty sir. But they were all in my
imagination.

LEO. What's the fun in that? Get yourself the real thing, man.

THOMAS. I'm in no hurry sir. The dreamer is happy with his
dreams.

EDGAR. What a sensible fellow. The dream is nearly always
better than the reality.

LEO. Hark at him, Thomas. And him only wed a month ago. I
tell you what, Thomas. Tell us some of your Granny's words
of wisdom. Surely she had some old saw for the advice of
newly weds?

THOMAS. Many, my lord. How about this one? "Man should
always be the master; woman's rule oft brings disaster".

LEO. Splendid, splendid. And it's true Edgar, it's quite true. Look
at my own case. *(sits, right)* I'm the master in my own house
and you couldn't find a happier marriage than ours.

EDGAR. You're greatly blessed, Leo.

LEO. "Woman's rule oft brings disaster". How true it is. You've
only to look around you.

THOMAS. Yes. Downstairs at this very moment . . .

LEO. What do you mean?

THOMAS. Why, there are six very unpleasant ladies downstairs, just waiting to rule your life and change your habits.

LEO. The League of Decency! I'd forgotten them.

EDGAR. *(sitting, left)* What's this?

LEO. It's a protest committee.

EDGAR. *(Laughing)* Of couse. It was inevitable.

LEO. It's all very well for you. What am I to say to them? Are they very angry, Thomas?

THOMAS. You bet they are. They were pretty vexed to start with and every hour of waiting increases their displeasure. They're sharpening themselves on each other, like knives before a good meal.

EDGAR. Tell us what they're saying.

THOMAS. Opinion seems to be divided as to who is more to blame, you, my lord, or Lady Godiva. A couple of them consider her ladyship a loose woman, but the rest of them say she is a helpless tool in her husband's grasp. It seems, sir, that you have besmirched the fair name of Coventry's womanhood.

LEO. besmirched?

THOMAS. Yes sir, begging your pardon. That word kept cropping up. It's a good word for sneering over, you see. It has a sort of indignant snarl, if you see what I mean. Besmirched.

EDGAR. *(trying it, with teeth bared wolfishly)* Besmirched.

LEO. *(Trying it, with mouth drawn down)* Besmirched.

EDGAR. Oh well, they can't go on feeling besmirched for ever. They'll get over it, you see, when they enjoy relief from their taxes.

THOMAS. Maybe they will, sir, but they mean to make things hot for his lordship. You see, they're afraid their daughters might want to follow Lady Godiva's example!

EDGAR. *(very much amused)* Oh glory! Think of it, Leo! A pageant of naked beauties, and all done in the name of charity!

LEO. *(rising in agitation)* Great Heavens, Edgar, it's no joke, to face a band of harridans who are out for your blood. I never dreamed I'd stir up such a hornet's nest. It seems a pity Old Moll couldn't have had a vision of *me* instead of my wife!

EDGAR. *(with a shout of laughter)* No, no, Leo, spare us that! Your hair's too short and your belly's too fat! Come, cheer up brother, *(rises)* You shan't face them alone. I'll fight for you till death. Two men should be able to vanquish six women.

THOMAS. Shall I come too, my lord?

LEO. No, Thomas. Stay here and if Godiva comes, ask her to wait for us. Shall we get it over then, Edgar?
(LEO and EDGAR go out, right. THOMAS wanders up and down, fidgetting and biting his nails.)

THOMAS. If Godiva comes, ask her to wait. If Godiva comes, ask her to wait. Dear God, let Godiva come. No, No, don't let her come; I should only make a fool of myself. Dear God, let her come and give me courage to say what I feel.
(He pretends to see GODIVA seated in chair, centre. He goes and kneels at left of it.)
Beautiful, adorable Godiva, what you did was brave and good and no committee of venomous old women can besmirch your virtue. If I could serve you, I'd be the happiest man alive.
(GODIVA enters at back and listens.)

THOMAS. Beautiful Godiva. Beautiful, beautiful Godiva, every man in Coventry is in love with you. Let me serve you and sit at your feet.

GODIVA. Whatever are you talking about?

THOMAS. *(scrambling to his feet and moving away, right)* Oh! My lady . . . . I was talking to myself.

GODIVA. *(smiling)* Indeed? I thought you were talking to me. I heard my name distinctly. *(comes down stage)* Did you not say Godiva?

THOMAS. I . . . . I may have done.

GODIVA. Perhaps you were practising a speech?

THOMAS. Er . . . yes. That's what I was doing.

GODIVA. Good. Now I am here you may say it to me in person. *(sits, centre)* What is your name, young man?

THOMAS. Thomas, my lady.

GODIVA. Well, Thomas, you have your audience. Begin your speech. *(THOMAS stares dumbly)* You were on your knees, I believe. *(He kneels. There is a pause)* Thomas, I'm waiting. *(He gulps)* Thomas, have you nothing to say?

THOMAS. My lady . . .I . . .You've taken me by surprise.

GODIVA. *(annoyed)* So it seems. You were eloquent when you thought you were alone.

THOMAS. Yes, my lady.

GODIVA, You were saying "beautiful Godiva". Start from there.

THOMAS. Beautiful Godiva . . . . . *(Pause)* I can't go on.

GODIVA. *(rising)* Oh, really, how provoking men are! What are you, anyway?

THOMAS. I'm a poet, my lady.

GODIVA. A poet? But you can't string two words together!

THOMAS. *(rising)* Oh yes I can. I've made up a poem about you.

GODIVA. About me? About yesterday?

THOMAS. Yes. His Lordship requested me to do so. I'm to say it to him this morning and if he likes it Cedric is to set it to music so that everyone will sing my words.

GODIVA. Well, well. So that's Leo's little plan. A charming thought. Yes, I shall like that, ... if it's any good.

THOMAS. It's the best thing I've ever done.

GODIVA. So you say. Let me hear it.

THOMAS. Oh, not yet, my lady. I'm to say it first to Lord Leofric.

GODIVA. Don't be ridiculous man. It's *about* me and it's *for* me, so kindly say it *to* me!

THOMAS. *(very distressed)* Please, my lady. I'd better not. His Lordship will be angry with me and I fear his wrath.

GODIVA. You cowardly little maggot! Don't you realise that if you offend me, his lordship will be even more furious?

THOMAS. Oh, I wish I.d never left the bakery!

GODIVA. Do you know what happens to people who offend Lord Leofric? They are cast into the prison dungeons and never seen again.

THOMAS. Never?

GODIVA. Never. They die there eventually, but it takes many years to die. Have you seen the dungeons, little man? It's dark down there, even at mid-day, and the floors are cold stone and water drips down the walls and the air is foul and and there is nothing to sit on and only rats for company.

THOMAS. Not rats!

GODIVA. Yes, rats. They'd make quite a meal off *you.*

THOMAS. Oh, no!

GODIVA. Some of the prisoners go mad, Thomas. Do you think *you* might go mad?

THOMAS. I'm half crazed with fear already. Oh, be merciful, Lady Godiva!
(He casts himself at her feet. CHRISTINA *enters at back and stands amazed.)*
Be merciful, I beg you!

GODIVA. Why should I?

THOMAS. Because I'm such a coward.

CHRIS. *(coming forward)* Why, what's this, Godiva?

GODIVA. *(with a laugh)* Oh, I was just having a little sport with this fellow and he was pretending to be frightened. Weren't you, Thomas?

THOMAS. Yes, my lady.

GODIVA. Well, get up man. The game is over *(THOMAS rises)* Christina, this is Thomas. He has written a poem about my ride and he won't let me hear it before Leo does. What would *you* do with the wretch?

CHRIS. I'd pretend I didn't want to hear it. I'd vow it mattered nothing to me.

GODIVA. As a matter of fact, that's true. I've lost all interest in the stupid poem. You can tell Leo, when he comes back, that I don't wish to hear it. *(She exits at back. THOMAS stares after her in dismay)*

THOMAS. But his lordship will be so upset if she refuses to hear it. What can I do?

CHRIS. Don't worry, Thomas. She'll hear it. Nothing on earth will prevent her.

THOMAS. You really think so.

CHRIS. Oh yes, I know Godiva. I should. I'm her sister.

THOMAS. Oh, I see! You must be the Lady Christina that Cedric was telling me about.

CHRIS. *(sitting centre)* Was he really? What did he tell you about me?

THOMAS. He said, when you were a little girl, he used to sit you on his knee and sing to you.

CHRIS. That's true. Cedric was my father's servant until Godiva married Leo and took Cedric along with her.

THOMAS. Did my lady Godiva ever sit on Cedric's knee?

CHRIS. No. She was too old for such childish nonsense.

THOMAS. I'm glad. I mean . . . well . . . . Cedric is a bit earthy, whereas she a . . . . a saint, in a way. Well, she *must* be, to do what she did. I wouldn't like to think of Cedric touching her. Nobody ought to touch her, from now on.

CHRIS. But if you admire her so much, why wouldn't you say
    her your poem? Has Leofric told you not to?
THOMAS. No.
CHRIS. Maybe it's unfit for women's ears?
THOMAS. *(indignantly)* It's perfectly fit. I don't make up *that*
    sort of stuff.
CHRIS. Then why?
THOMAS. I don't know. She seemed so different from what I'd
    expected, somehow.
CHRIS. Different?
THOMAS. I never saw her close to, before today. I thought she'd
    be . . . . .gentler. More like you. It must have been something
    about me that annoyed her. You mustn't think there was any
    fault on her side. There couldn't be. She's faultless.
CHRIS. *(gently)* Poor Thomas. You're in love with her.
THOMAS. Yes. Do you wonder? Every man in Coventry is in
    love with her, since yesterday. Such goodness and courage and
    beauty, all in one woman. It's incredible.
CHRIS. *(kindly)* You must have written a very beautiful poem
    about her, feeling as you do.
THOMAS. Yes, it is beautiful. I wish the earl would come back, so
    that I could say it to him. My brain is so full of it, I can think
    of nothing else.
CHRIS. Would you like to say it to me?
THOMAS. *(after a pause for consideration)* Yes, I think I would.
    May I?
CHRIS. I should be honoured.
THOMAS. It's a good idea. Then I shan't be nervous next time.
CHRIS. Are you nervous now?
THOMAS. I shall be, if you look at me. You have such
    expressive eyes. Please don't look at me.
    (She faces front. THOMAS wanders about, tries leaning over

the chair on the right, changes his mind and eventually ends
up by the window, leaning on the wall for support. He says
his poem quietly and with strong feeling.
THOMAS. Ride forth, fair warrior. No trumpets cry,
  No banners wave, no armour blazes bright;
  Only a horse's mild, unheedful eye
  Turns at the solemn, sweet, forbidden sight.
  Above all horses he most truly blessed,
  Led by her touch, by her soft hand caressed.

  No jewelled gown bedecks her lovely form
  No mantle lined with silk and edged with fur
  Circles her slender arms to keep them warm:
  The morning breeze makes gentle sport with her.
  Yet never was a queen more dazzling fair
  Than she beneath her cloak of raven hair.
  (CHRISTINA listens with obvious pleasure till at the last line
  her eyes open wide with alarm. There is a pause. He is waiting
  for her comment. She is wondering what to say.
CHRIS. Thomas, was this poem written from imagination?
THOMAS. Yes, my lady.
CHRIS. You never saw my sister before today?
THOMAS. No, my lady. Is there something wrong?
CHRIS. Only a small thing. It's a wonderful poem Thomas . . .
  but the last line isn't true.
THOMAS. "Than she beneath her cloak of raven hair"?
CHRIS. Yes. You see, my sister has golden hair. You'd better
  alter it before you say it to Leo. You couldn't have known, of
  course. The modern style of head-dress makes it quite
  impossible to see what colour . . . .
THOMAS. *(coming down right)* Lady Godiva has golden hair?
CHRIS. Yes., beautiful pale golden hair. She's very proud of it.

You'll just have to alter . . . .

THOMAS. It *wasn't* golden. It *wasn't*.

CHRIS. *(rising)* What are you saying?

THOMAS. It wasn't golden yesterday.

(CHRISTINA goes to him and grips his arm.

CHRIS. How do you know? Answer me, how do you know?

THOMAS. *(very low)* I saw.

CHRIS. *(drawing away, horrified)* You were looking?

THOMAS. I wanted to write such a splendid poem. I was afraid my imagination might fail me. I barred my window just as I'd been told and sat in the darkened room listening for the sound of her horse's hooves on the cobbles. At last I heard her approaching. I opened the shutters just a little way and peered through the crack. I saw her pass beneath me. I couldn't see her face but her hair was as black as . . . . *(he pauses and stares at her)* . . . as black as yours

CHRIS. As black as mine! *(She clasps first her long braids and then her cheeks as if to hide her blushes. She turns away and sinks on to bench, left. THOMAS sits on chair, down right, looking miserable.)*

THOMAS. Why? Why didn't she . . . . ?

CHRIS. She was afraid. She was more than afraid. She was on the point of collapse. Someone had to go: the alternative was too shameful. Leofric would have been so humiliated. It was for his sake, as well as for hers.

THOMAS. Yes, of course, someone had to go. But, what about the nuns?

CHRIS. They were under a vow not to raise their eyes from the ground. We had to take that risk, and Margery was sworn to secrecy. Who would have dreamed that *you* would dare to look out. *(rises in agitation)* You mustn't tell! Do you understand? You must never tell!

THOMAS. My God, is it likely?

CHRIS. *(hardly listening)* It isn't only a matter of pride. It isn't just that Leofric and Godiva would be held up to public ridicule. That would be bad enough but he is so proud of her, Thomas. It would hurt him terribly, to know she had failed him. Promise me on you word of honour. that you will keep this secret.

THOMAS. What do you take me for, a hero? Would I admit with my own lips that I had disobeyed the earl's command and opened my window to see his lady ride by with no clothes on? Don't you know what the punishment for that is? Prison for life. Prison for the rest of my days . . . . and I'm very young so there'd be a lot of days. I've pictured it so often, I seem to know already how it feels. I can feel the cold iron chafing my wrists and ankles and the cold stone under my scraggy bottom. I can hear the rats squeaking and rustling, and smell the foul damp air all around me. And I can feel the ache of hunger in my belly and the awful despair in my heart. Oh, heaven preserve me from it! *(He buries his face in his hands.* CHRISTINA *looks at him with pity)*

CHRIS. Poor Thomas. I see I need not have demanded your vow of secrecy. But if it's any comfort I give you mine. No-one shall hear from *my* lips what *you* did.

THOMAS. *(looking up at her)* Not even your husband?

CHRIS. *(turning away)* Least of all my husband.

THOMAS. Haven't you told him?

CHRIS. I've told him nothing. He wouldn't understand. He thinks the whole idea is shameful and degrading.

THOMAS. Oh, it wasn't! *(rising)* It was beautiful and uplifting. How could any man think otherwise?

CHRIS. *(sadly)* Not all men are like you, Thomas.

THOMAS. *(humbly)* May I kiss your hand, my lady? *(He kneels *and she lets him kiss her hand)* If I could serve you I'd be the happiest man alive.

CHRIS. *(smiling)* Fickle wretch. A minute ago you loved Godiva.

THOMAS. *(rising)* No, it was never Godiva. It was the heroine on horseback that I loved and nothing has changed that.

CHRIS. Never the less, it is to Godiva's household you will belong, once the earl has heard your charming poem. You won't forget to alter the last line will you?

THOMAS. I won't forget, my lady. My freedom depends on it.
  (Enter LEOFRIC and EDGAR, right. LEO collapses in centre chair.)

LEO. Oh, the saints preserve me from ever going through that again. I'd rather face a boatload of Danes.

CHRIS. Why Leo, where have you been?

LEO. Christina, we have received a protest committee from the League of Decency and they have reduced me to a pulp. I've lost every shred of self-respect. Get me a drink, for pity's sake. *(She hurries to fetch pitcher and cup from table.)*

THOMAS. Did they say you'd besmirched them?

LEO. They did, repeatedly. And worse. I began to fear they'd tear me limb from limb. Luckily this brave fellow intervened and saved me.

CHRIS. What did you do, Edgar?

EDGAR. *(sitting down, right)* All I did was take down their complaints in writing. It worked like a charm. They seemed quite overcome at the thought of their words being written down on parchment.

LEO. They looked at Edgar with such awe and reverence that I let him do all the talking. It was deucedly clever, the way he managed to seem to be on their side.

EDGAR. *(with a warning look)* I *am* on their side, Leo.

LEO. *(taking cup and drinking)* Thanks, Christina. Oh, it was vastly amusing, really. The more I think of it, the more it tickles me. And Thomas, what do you think? One of them asked how they could prevent their daughters following Godiva's example, and d'you know what this fellow said? Eh? He said, "Cut off their hair"! *(laughes loudly)* Quick as a flash. "Cut off their hair". You should have seen their faces. *(LEO gets an angry glance from* EDGAR*)*

EDGAR. Leo, for heaven's sake! I gave them good advice. If young women didn't wear their hair so long this would never have happened.

LEO. *(More subdued)* True, true. You'd better watch out, Christina, or he'll chop off your long braids while you're asleep.

EDGAR. I don't think I need bother, in Christina's case. What do you think, my love?

CHRIS. I don't understand. What are you asking me, Edgar?

EDGAR. Is there any chance of your following Godiva's example?

CHRIS. Chance? I . . . . . I hardly suppose . . . .

EDGAR. *(gently)* Come here, now. *(takes her hand)* Heavens, why are you trembling? I'm not angry with you. I only asked if *you* could ever do such a thing as your sister did?

CHRIS. *(hopefully)* Would you want me to, Edgar?

EDGAR. *(embarrassed)* You know me better than that. Of course I would never ask you to do such a thing. But all the same, if it were to save a life, eh?

CHRIS. *(uncertain how to answer)* I can't imagine such a situation arising.

LEO. Neither can I. But I bet she could do it just for the fun of it. Eh, Christina? What did Godiva say; she enjoyed feeling the free winds of heaven on every part of her body. Don't you think you'd feel like that?

CHRIS. *(taking fright at hearing her own words)* No, Leo! That

was Godiva, not me! I couldn't have said that. I wouldn't feel
like that. I . . . . I wish you wouldn't keep on about it!
*(She dashes out, down left. LEO shrugs. EDGAR gives a
gesture of despair.)*
EDGAR. You see what I mean? I might just as well be married to
a nun, a beautiful, childlike nun. Oh, Uncle Steven, what have
you done!
LEO. Thank goodness Uncle Steven never got his clutches on
Godiva.
(Enter LADY HILDA, at back.)
HILDA. Leo, what's this I hear? We are to be entertained by some
strolling player?
LEO. Not exactly. But come and sit down, mother. We are to
hear a poem by this young man, Thomas.
*(HILDA seats herself, down right. THOMAS, who has been
tactfully keeping out of sight, comes forward and bows.*
HILDA. Thomas? are you not a strolling player?
THOMAS. No, my lady. I'm a baker my lady.
HILDA. A baker?
THOMAS. Yes, my lady. But I'm not as half-baked as I look.
(HILDA glares. LEO frowns.)
LEO. Thomas, lad, I'd rather you didn't try to be funny. It's
always so embarrassing. You're much better at your sad
poems.
HILDA. We are to hear a sad poem today?
LEO. About Godiva's wonderful ride, mother.
HILDA. So you admit that it was a sad day for this family when . .
LEO. No, no, I should have said serious. Not sad; serious.
HILDA. And how does this youth know so much about a sight
which no man was supposed to see?
LEO. Because Thomas has that wonderful gift, imagination. He
has only to shut his eyes and he can see it all quite clearly.

HILDA. Oh, don't tell me any more. It's all too plain, Leo. Your house is cluttered up with scheming villains who claim to be able to see what ordinary mortals can't. When will you realise that they are making a fool of you?

EDGAR. My dear mother-in-law, this young man is quite different from Old Moll.

HILDA. I can see that he is younger and cleaner, thank heaven. That woman smells abominably. I hope you weren't thinking of inviting her to this entertainment. I can't bear her within five yards of me. She makes me feel . . . .*(she gropes for a suitable word)*

LEO, EDGAR and THOMAS. Besmirched?

HILDA. *(surprised)* Exactly! *(They laugh)* Well, enjoy your little joke, whatever it may be, and then listen to this. I went down past the stables just now and I found that the horse on which Godiva rode has had its tail and its mane cut off!

LEO. Cut off!

HILDA. Completely. I never saw a more undignified beast.

LEO. *(furious)* But this is sheer vandalism. It's these women, the League of Decency! This is their answer to your advice, Edgar.

EDGAR. My advice?

LEO. Yes. Cut off their hair, you said, and so they've done this. The wicked old harridans. I'll put them in the stocks. They shan't get away with it. My best horse! *(crosses to exit, right)*

THOMAS. *(running to stop him)* Stop, sir! Stop! You're wrong!

LEO. *(turning)* Wrong? What do you know about it?

THOMAS. It must have been done before the Protest Committee appeared. I think it was done in the night, sir.

LEO. How do you know?

THOMAS. Because in the first light of dawn I heard men calling on the street corner, selling hairs from Godiva's horse, a penny a hair. They were doing a brisk trade, too. Sold out in twenty minutes.

LEO. *(extremely impressed)* A penny for a hair from Godiva's horse? They must have made a small fortune. Did you hear that, Edgar? A penny a hair. What enterprise! Did you see who the wretches were, Thomas?

THOMAS. No, my lord. It was barely daylight.

LEO. Sold out in twenty minutes! But see here, they could cut the tail off *any* white horse and sell it. Simple folk will believe anything. They could grow rich on Godiva's ride! There's money to be made out of this and the people of Coventry aren't slow to realise it. First the alchemist, then the horse barber. What next, I wonder?

THOMAS. The silver smith, sir.

LEO. Yes, what about him?

THOMAS. He intends to ask permission to make silver medals, depicting Lady Godiva on her horse, and sell them as souvenirs.

LEO. Souvenirs? Oh, I can't allow that. Not my wife's image, sold on the streets.

THOMAS. He was going to offer you half his profits, sir.

LEO. Was he, indeed? Hm, I must think about it.

HILDA. *(repressively)* Naturally you couldn't allow a picture of your wife's naked person.

LEO. No, no, of course not mother. I wouldn't dream of it.

HILDA. However, if in this picture her hair were carefully arranged . . . . . .

LEO. So that nothing showed! Of course!

HILDA. You would insist that he submitted a specimen for your approval, of course.

LEO. Mother, you're a wonder! *(He leans admiringly on the back of her chair.* THOMAS *is now below* HILDA, *right)*

HILDA. And you'd need to keep a careful check on his sales to

make sure you were getting your share. Edgar, you could see
to that. You're good at keeping accounts.

EDGAR. *(uncertainly)* I don't know that the bishop would
approve.

HILDA. The bishop need know nothing about it!

EDGAR. You mean it? Well, in that case . . . . .
> *(He comes over and squats beside HILDA. All four begin to
> look like conspirators.)*

Why not get six women dressed as nuns and a white horse
that hasn't been trimmed, and let them journey up and down
the country collecting money in the name of charity.

HILDA. For *charity*, Edgar?

EDGAR. Well, *half* of it could go to charity.

HILDA. Edgar, there's more in you than meets the eye.

EDGAR. And in you too. Lady Hilda.

LEO. What a woman! Now I really can believe that you defaced
those holy pictures in your childhood.

HILDA. Yes. I was entirely to blame, of course. Steven only came
along to try and prevent me.

EDGAR. He can't have tried very hard.

HILDA. Not after I hit him with a censer!
> *(She permits herself a tight smile while the men laugh. As they
> are enjoying the joke, GODIVA and CHRISTINA enter at the
> back.)*

GODIVA. *(peevishly)* Well, Leo, have I to wait all day to hear
this poem?

LEO. What poem? Oh yes, *that* poem. I didn't know you knew
about it.

GODIVA. *(coming down)* Oh, that creature couldn't wait to tell
me.

LEO. *(reproachfully)* Thomas.

THOMAS. I'm sorry, sir. But I didn't say it to her, not without you hearing it first.

GODIVA. *(sitting, centre)* Foolish fellow, nobody cares who you say it to first. Only for goodness sake, get on with it. Leo, come and sit here, on my right side. Edgar, on my left. *(EDGAR sits on her left, on edge of dais)*

GODIVA. Christina, you'd better stand behind mother. *(CHRISTINA crosses and stands behind HILDA)* You stand there Thomas, or whatever your name is. *(THOMAS goes to a position down left)* Leo!

LEO. *(in a reverie)* A penny for a hair!

GODIVA. My dear Leo, you sound half-witted today. I told you to come and sit here.

LEO. *(surprised at her tone)* Told me?

GODIVA. Yes. Don't stand there gaping. I don't know which is more trying, you or this stupid baker's boy who thinks he's a poet.

HILDA. He may be a baker's boy, Godiva, but he's not half-baked. *(LEO goes and sits on dais beside GODIVA)* Now, young man, we're ready for you to begin. Are you word perfect?

THOMAS. *(nervously)* I hope so, my lady.

LEO. Mind you speak up, boy. I can't bear mumblers.

THOMAS. Yes, my lord.

GODIVA. It's rather cool in this room. I wonder if you'd fetch me a cloak, Edgar? *(EDGAR begins to rise)*

HILDA. Godiva! You managed yesterday without a cloak. It's a bit late to feel the draught now!

GODIVA. Oh, very well. Get on with it, boy.

(A short pause. THOMAS is biting his nails nervously)

GODIVA. Leo, if you didn't breathe so heavily I might be able to hear.

LEO. *(losing patience)* There's nothing *to* hear yet! Thomas, if

you don't begin your confounded verses this instant, I'll throw
you out of the window!

THOMAS. Yes, sir. It's just that I can't seem to remember.

LEO. *(noisily)* You can't remember!

CHRIS. Thomas, don't be nervous. I'm sure it's a wonderful poem.

THOMAS. *(frantically)* I can't remember anything but the last
line!

GODIVA. Well, of all the ridiculous . . . . .

HILDA. *(decisively)* Young man, you must clear your head. Take
a deep breath, shut your eyes and count slowly up to ten.
*(He does so. As he begins, silently, MARGERY runs in at
right and opens her mouth but HILDA turns and raises hand)*

HILDA. Silence!
*(MARGERY runs to LEO and whispers in his ear. LEO starts
up in alarm)*

LEO. What?

HILDA. Hush!
*(LEO hurries out. MARGERY whispers to GODIVA, who
runs to window, then out, followed by MARGERY. CHRIS
and EDGAR run to window, then beckon to HILDA who
rises unwillingly. As THOMAS reaches ten, all three are
beginning to go, right.*

THOMAS. I remember now. Oh!
(His face falls. So does the CURTAIN.)

CURTAIN.

ACT THREE

The same. That afternoon. LEOFRIC is seated, down right, moodily biting his nails. GODIVA is staring angrily out of the window.

GODIVA. What a scene you made of yourself. What a ridiculous, shameful scene!

LEO. It's all very well complaining, Godiva, but what would you have done?

GODIVA. *(coming down centre)* I?

LEO. Yes, what would you have done? There I was with half a dozen screaming girls all clinging round my legs and begging for protection, and surrounded on all sides by angry mothers, armed to the teeth with ugly-looking knives.

GODIVA. Well, what did you expect? You told them to cut off their daughters' hair.

LEO. I did nothing of the sort. That was Edgar's idea.

GODIVA. You gave it your approval.

LEO. I never thought they'd try it, though. Ye Gods, you have to be careful what you say to women. I was petrified.

GODIVA. That was only too obvious. *(goes and sits, down left)* I felt downright ashamed of you, the brave Earl Leofric, shaking like a leaf.

LEO. *(rising)* I deny that I was shaking.

GODIVA. Oh yes, you were. I could hear your teeth chattering.

LEO. Godiva. don't exaggerate. When twelve women all talk

at once you can't hear a donkey bray.

GODIVA. *(nastily)* Indeed? So that's why you couldn't make yourself heard.

LEO. *(hurt)* Godiva, please try to understand. I'm brave enough when I'm up against men, but these were women . . . six gentle, helpless young creatures crying out to me to save them, and six good ladies of high virtue exhorting me to discipline their erring daughters. Whatever I did I would hurt *somebody* and it isn't manly to hurt a woman.

GODIVA. It isn't very manly to scream "Help!" and have to be rescued by your mother-in-law. *(LEO is overcome with shame)* If mother hadn't intervened, there'd have been a massacre!

LEO. *(humbly)* She was wonderful. When she raised her voice, those awful women just quailed before her. She's a brave woman . . . . just like her daughter.

GODIVA. *(startled)* Like Christina? What do you mean?

LEO. *(going to her)* Silly girl, I meant *you*, the wonderful woman who rode the white horse yesterday . . .or had you forgotten?

GODIVA. *(with a laugh)* Oh, that. That was nothing. I'd do it again tomorrow.

LEO. I'm glad to hear you say that. The tradesmen want to know if it's going to be an annual event.

GODIVA. *(horrified)* No! Certainly not! I couldn't possibly!

LEO. But you just said . . . .

GODIVA. *(floundering)* Well . . . . it isn't that I'd *mind* . . . it's just that, well, if you keep *on* doing a thing, people aren't impressed any more. That sort of thing should only happen once in a lifetime.

LEO. Ah, how wise you are, my love.

(OLD MOLL *wanders in at back and finds a chicken leg under the table. She sits on floor and starts to gnaw the bone.)*

What did you think of Thomas's poem, eh? Pretty good, wasn't it?

GODIVA. I didn't like it very much. It was more about the *horse* than me.

LEO. Well, *he* was naked too, you know!

GODIVA. *(jumping up angrily)* Leo! How can you! You're trying to belittle my sacrifice.

LEO. *(putting arm round her shoulder)* Oh no, darling, never. You were absolutely wonderfully brave and Thomas shouldn't have wasted his talents on the horse.

GODIVA. I should think not, great awkward animal, and bad-tempered too.

LEO. Buster bad-tempered? Oh no, you couldn't find a more amiable horse in the whole of Coventry.

GODIVA. Indeed? Then let me tell you that half-way up Market Street he tried to toss me!

LEO. Half-way up where?

GODIVA. Market Street.

LEO. Impossible.

GODIVA. Oh, I knew you wouldn't believe it. Your precious Buster can do no wrong.

LEO. He *can* do wrong . . . . but not half way up Market Street! All this week they've had the road up and traffic has been diverted round Church Lane.

GODIVA. *(confused)* Oh, well, I *meant* Church Lane. Is it any wonder that I'm confused after going through such an ordeal? *(Enter* CHRISTINA *at back)* I wonder that you dare to keep picking on *me*, after the performance *you* gave this morning. If the king of France wants to invade England, he only needs to send an army of women and it'll be over in five minutes!

CHRISTINA. Godiva, there are a couple of nuns in the courtyard . .

GODIVA. *(waspishly)* Well, don't let them come near Leo or he'll have a fit! *(LEO, goaded beyond endurance, grits his teeth and exits, right)* What do they want, these nuns?

CHRIS. Well, you know that the Mother Superior runs sewing classes for the housewives?

GODIVA. Yes?

CHRISTINA. She wants to know if you'll come and give them a talk.

GODIVA. Me? Give a talk?

CHRIS. A talk on dress.

GODIVA. *(after staring at her for a moment)* She must be joking!

CHRIS. *(giggling)* I don't think so. She hasn't got much sense of humour.

GODIVA. *(turning towards audience)* Ladies, up till recently it has been fashionable to wear clothes, but this year I am introducing an entirely new fashion . . . . . *(They both laugh)* But seriously, what on earth can I give a talk about? I don't know the first thing about sewing.

CHRIS. I shouldn't think they want to hear about sewing. You could describe all the latest styles and the new materials that are coming over from France. You could take a few of your favourite gowns and put them on and slink up and down with your toes turned out.

GODIVA. The Mother Superior wouldn't like that.

CHRIS. I bet she would. She's a woman, isn't she? And you could tell them which colours are fashionable and which are out of date.

GODIVA. Which *are* out of date?

CHRIS. Well, I hear that blue isn't being worn much this year.

GODIVA. Really? I hadn't heard. *(looks round at MOLL)* Moll, that cloak you're wearing . . . . it's terribly tattered. In fact, quite beyond mending.

MOLL. Is it, dearie? I've never tried.

GODIVA. Never mind. I've an old blue one that's in quite good condition and you can have *that* if you wish. *(She smiles very graciously)* Go and tell Margery to give it you. It's the one with the silver clasp.

MOLL. *(rising, grinning toothlessly)* Silver clasp, eh? Old Moll with a silver clasp! Wait till you see me in all my finery. You won't know me next time, I'll be that grand. *(Exit at back)*

GODIVA. Poor old woman.

CHRIS. She gives me the creeps. I don't trust her.

GODIVA. Oh, I do. She's devoted to me.

CHRIS. *(meaningly)* So is Leo.

GODIVA. What's that supposed to mean?

CHRIS. Leo is far more devoted to you than that false old hag. But what do you give *him?*

GODIVA. Give him? I don't have to give him anything. He's my husband.

CHRIS. Yes, he *is* your husband. One would have thought he was a scullion, to hear you talk to him this afternoon.

GODIVA. It's no business of yours how I talk to him. *(rises and crosses left)*

CHRIS. Look Godiva, I'm fond of Leo. Up till yesterday I thought you were too. But ever since that cursed ride you've been different.

GODIVA. I know I have. I can't help it. I *feel* different. I used to be so spineless and stupid and afraid of what people thought of me. It never occured to me to question anything that Leo said. I was utterly negative. But suddenly I'm a different woman. I'm important. I'm admired. I'm probably unique. You just have to be a positive personality when people know you rode naked through the streets.

CHRIS. *(exploding)* But you *didn't!*

GODIVA. *(calmly)* I know. And you know. But no-one else does.

CHRIS. Margery does.

GODIVA. Oh, Margery . . . . she'll keep quiet. Her mother and
father depend on us utterly for their livelihood.
CHRIS. What makes you so sure *I'll* keep quiet?
GODIVA. Because you're so fond of Leo. The truth would break
Leo's heart. You won't tell him.
CHRIS. *(turning away with a sigh)* No, I won't tell him. But for
heaven's sake, why can't you be nicer to him?
GODIVA. Oh, you make too much of a few thoughtless words. I
make it up to him a hundredfold in private. You know what
married people are like, or if you don't you ought to. Haven't
you ever quarrelled with Edgar and made it up when you went
to bed? *(CHRISTINA shakes her head)* Oh, I forgot. Your
husband only loves you like a brother. You know Christina,
it's about time you did something about that. Well, it stands
to reason, any woman who knows her job can rouse a bit of
the old Adam, even in a cold fish like Edgar. I bet *I* could.
He's really rather attractive . . . . . that pale, monastic calm . . .
CHRIS. *(turning to her)* Godiva, I'd rather not discuss . . .
*(She stops as EDGAR enters at back. She turns and runs out,
right.)*
EDGAR. *(advancing)* Oh, she's gone. Is something wrong?
GODIVA. She seems a little edgy lately, don't you find?
EDGAR. Edgy? I hadn't noticed it. I was going to ask her to
get a splinter out of my hand.
GODIVA. I'll do it for you. Come and sit down here beside me.
*(She sits, down right. He crosses and crouches beside her,
left of her chair)*
EDGAR. I've been trying to get it out with this needle, but I
can't seem to do anything with my left hand.
GODIVA. Give me the needle. Now, let's have a look at this
splinter. *(He shows his right hand)* Why, it's quite deep. You'll
have to come closer if I'm to get at that. *(he moves his hand a*

little) Oh, come now, I meant *much* closer. I just can't see what I'm doing at that distance. *(she draws his whole arm on to her lap)* That's better. Anyone would think you were shy of being touched.

EDGAR. Oh no, of course not.

GODIVA. *(starting to probe splinter)* I wouldn't laugh at you if you were. A young man like you, brought up in the church, leads such a sheltered life. Getting married can be just as much an ordeal for a shy man as for a woman, I should think. But you soon get used to it.

EDGAR. Get used to what?

GODIVA. Well, you know . . . . . being a husband. Being on intimate terms with a woman. At first you have to try and forget your shyness; put on a bold front, as they say. And then stop thinking of women as something too frail to touch. We're not, you know — we're quite tough, and we don't like being kept at a distance.

EDGAR. Don't you? *(He is puzzled by this conversation and rather wary)*

GODIVA. Oh no. Why, if this were Leo having a splinter removed, I expect I'd be sitting on his knee and he'd have his head on my . . . . . my shoulder, and it would be as pleasant and comfortable as can be. That's how married people ought to be. But you and Christina will never be like that if you don't get over your shyness. Now, I know what the trouble is; you just haven't had any experience.

EDGAR. Experience?

GODIVA. Of women. *(She looks at him meaningly for a moment, then goes back to the splinter. EDGAR flinches with a look of pain)*

GODIVA. Am I hurting you?

EDGAR. *(bravely)* No, not at all.

GODIVA. I'm trying so hard to be gentle. I know, lay your head against my knee and don't look what I'm doing. *(He hesitates)* Go on, it's all right. Make yourself nice and comfortable and relax. *(He gingerly leans his head against her knee. She strokes his hair)*
What thick hair you have. And your hands are wonderfully long and sensitive. *(goes on working at splinter)* Don't you think that hands tell us an awful lot about people? Now, yours for instance, thin and strong, square at the finger tips and rather hairy.

EDGAR. And what does that tell you?

GODIVA. I think you're a person of strong emotions, well controlled. I think that although you look outwardly cold, you're inwardly rather passionate.
(EDGAR snatches his hand away and jumps up, moving away left.)

EDGAR. You see far too much, Godiva.

GODIVA. *(running to him and grasping his arm)* Oh, forgive me, Edgar. I know I'm too outspoken. It's just that I can't bear to see you being starved of a little warmth. You can't deny it. Your face gets thinner every day and I have to watch you withering up for want of a little womanly affection . . . .and all because you're afraid to make the first move. *(She puts her hands on his chest and looks up appealingly)* But you don't have to be shy with me, Edgar. I know so well what a man wants and you're no different from all the rest, if you'd only let yourself go. It's easy. It really is. I could show you, Edgar, if you'd let me.
(For a moment he is tempted, then he shuts his eyes)

EDGAR. Godiva, if we are to continue this conversation, please take your hands off my chest. *(She does so, but remains very close. He opens his eyes)* Now take three paces backwards.

GODIVA. *(retreating)* I've shocked you.

EDGAR. Why should I be shocked? You are a person who follows her heart both in words and actions. Not many of us have the courage to do that.

GODIVA. *(moving to him again)* Edgar, my dear. . . . .

EDGAR. No, stay where you are. Believe me, Godiva, I'm very grateful to you for trying to help me sort out my marriage, but I don't really think your remedy is the right one. I've no idea what Christina has been telling you, but I prefer to work out my problem for myself. And if you don't mind, I'll keep my splinter, too.

GODIVA. *(pettishly)* Oh, very well, go on acting like a monk. No wonder you drive Christina to desperation. And here's your needle, but you won't draw any blood with it, because there's only ice-water in your veins!
(She throws the needle angrily on the floor and sits down right. EDGAR goes down on his knees to hunt for needle. Enter LEO and THOMAS at back.)

LEO. Hello, Edgar. Saying your prayers?

EDGAR. *(rising with dignity)* I'd dropped something.
(He sits on bench, left, and fiddles uselessly with splinter. LEO crosses to GODIVA and kisses top of her head.)

LEO. Feeling better, dear?

GODIVA. I wasn't aware that I'd been ill.

LEO. Just a little out of sorts, my love. Only natural after what you went through yesterday.

GODIVA. Yesterday! I'm sick of hearing about yesterday. Can't anyone talk of anything else?

LEO. But, my dear, there's nothing else worth talking of.

GODIVA. Then for pity's sake, shut up!
(LEO retires, hurt, and stands at back with THOMAS. A commotion is heard, off, and CHRISTINA appears at back

holding a wailing, struggling OLD MOLL *who is dressed in unusually fine raiment:- an embroidered dress and a blue cloak with a silver clasp.*

CHRIS. *(dragging her forward)* Look at this, Godiva! Look what I found in my room! Look what the creature's wearing!

MOLL. You said I could have it, dearie. Didn't you say I could have the blue cloak?

GODIVA. Yes, I did. And you heard me, Christina, so why all the fuss?

CHRIS. It's not the cloak, it's the dress. My very best embroidered dress!

MOLL. I never meant to keep it. I only wanted to try it. I was just going to put it back.

CHRIS. And do you think I could ever wear it after *you*, you filthy old wretch? How dare you try on my clothes! How dare you!

GODIVA. Stop shouting, Christina, it makes my head ache. Old Moll was naughty to try on your dress, but surely you could afford to give it to her? I thought you were more charitable.

CHRIS. Charitable? I only give charity to deserving cases. And I won't have my hand forced into giving my best dress to a dirty common thief!

MOLL. *(drawing herself up)* I deny that I'm a thief. Can you deny that you're a loose woman?

(There is a sudden silence.)

GODIVA. What did you say?

MOLL. Can she deny that she's a loose woman?

LEO. *(coming forward)* Old Moll, you forget yourself!

MOLL. Oh no, I don't. I kept my mouth shut and told myself it was no concern of mine, what a fine lady does behind her husband's back. But when she calls me a thief in front of everyone, it's time to speak out. She's a loose woman. Ask

her what she was doing yesterday, when Godiva was riding
through Coventry.

EDGAR. *(coming forward)* Old woman, be careful what you say.
If you blacken my wife's character out of sheer malice, you'll
find yourself in the deepest dungeon of Coventry's prison.

MOLL. I can't blacken something that's black with sin already.
Ask her where she was. Go on, ask her!

EDGAR. I will not ask her. I know my wife has done no wrong.

MOLL. Then I'll ask her. Where were you, my fine lady, and
what were you doing?

CHRIS. I won't answer you. I don't have to answer to the likes
of you.

LEO. Certainly not. Moll, you will apologise instantly and go to
the kitchen at once.

MOLL. I will not apologise and if I go to the kitchen I'll come
back with Cedric.

LEO. Cedric? What does Cedric know about it?

MOLL. He was with her. In her room.

CHRIS. It's a lie! I was up on the ramparts, alone.

LEO. There you are, Moll. You were mistaken.

EDGAR. No, Leo. *I* was up on the ramparts, and *I* was alone.
Christina, why did you say you were there? Were you really
with Cedric?

CHRIS. *(nervously)* I did speak with Cedric, for a few moments,
at the door of our room. We are old friends, you see. I hadn't
seen him for months.

MOLL. *(laughing)* Old friends, indeed! They must have had a lot
to tell each other. They were in that room for a whole hour,
whispering and giggling. I heard her say, "Bolt the door,
Cedric" and I heard him do so. *(She crosses down left,
grinning)*

EDGAR. Christina, is this true?

CHRIS. Can you believe this old woman before me?

EDGAR. Not if you deny it.

CHRIS. I do deny it. I was . . . . . somewhere else.

EDGAR. Where were you?

CHRIS. I can't tell you. Godiva, help me!

GODIVA. How can I help you? I was riding down the streets with other things on my mind. *I* don't know where you were. I wouldn't blame you if you *were* making love to Cedric. He's got a bit more life in him than that cold fish you married . . . and you said you were desperate!

CHRIS. Godiva, how could you!

THOMAS. My lady, how could you!

LEO. You keep out of this, Thomas.

EDGAR. So it's true! Your whole manner gives you away! Why else should you blush and stammer and refuse to answer? God, how blind I've been!

CHRIS. *(pitifully)* Edgar, not in front of all these people.

EDGAR. Why not? You've shown me up in front of them; now you can share my shame. Oh, you've deceived us all wonderfully with your sweet modest ways. How easily we were all taken in . . . . . Uncle Steven, your mother, your sister and me most of all. To think that I held back, time and time again, even though I had the right, because I thought you were too young and innocent, only to find that you could give yourself to a servant!
(She is too shaken with tears to deny it. She can only shake her head.)
To think that I refused the advances of another woman, because I loved you and thought you loved me!

CHRIS. I do, Edgar, I do! *(She clasps his arm but he throws her off)*

EDGAR. Don't touch me! For weeks I've longed for you to

touch me but you held yourself aloof. Now I know how cheap
your embraces are I no longer want them. I'll have no more to
do with you. Go back to your lover and be thankful I don't
have you put in the stocks! Get out of my way, I never want
to see you again!

(He makes for back exit but finds THOMAS *firmly planted
in his way.)*

THOMAS. Please sir, don't go. There's something you don't know.

EDGAR. And I don't want to know. Let me pass.

THOMAS. *(grabbing him)* You *shall* know!

EDGAR. Take your hands off me.

THOMAS. Then listen to me. Your wife is innocent!

CHRIS. Thomas, you mustn't!

THOMAS. I must. I can't keep quiet any longer.

CHRIS. Thomas, don't be a fool. For your own sake as well as
   for hers.

THOMAS. What do I care for her sake? She's no good. She sat
   there and wouldn't raise a finger to help you.

CHRIS. Her hands are tied.

GODIVA. Christina, what is this man saying? What does he know?

CHRIS. Everything.

LEO. For heaven's sake, will somebody please explain what is
   going on. Thomas, if you can prove Christina's innocence, I
   command you to do so.

GODIVA. Thomas, if you drag me into this I'll have your tongue
   cut out!

THOMAS. *(after an appalled silence)* That's not a nice prospect
   for someone whose only talent is for babbling poetry . . . . .
   but it isn't such good poetry as all that. Perhaps a few words
   of truth are worth all the bad verses I could make in a
   lifetime. *(He addresses* EDGAR *without any attempt at drama)*
   Sir, during the time in question your wife was riding on a

white horse round the streets of Coventry. She had with her
six nuns and not a stitch of clothing. She did it to save the
face of her sister Godiva, whose courage failed her at the last
moment. *(He turns to* LEO*)* I know this, my lord, because
against your command I looked out of my window as she rode
by. The woman who passed beneath my window had black
hair, but I called it golden in my poem so as not to give away
the secret. Now I am ready to go to prison.
*(*LEO *sits, centre, looking stunned.* GODIVA *hides her face
in her hands.* EDGAR *is towards centre back.* CHRISTINA
goes to* THOMAS, *centre front.)*

CHRIS. Thomas, you're the bravest, most chivalrous man I know.
But I'm afraid your gallant confession only gets me out of the
frying pan into the fire. The sort of woman who rides naked
through the streets is worse in my husband's eyes than the
sort who . . . . .

EDGAR. *(rushing forward)* No, by God! The sort of woman
who could do that is the sort of woman I'm proud to be
married to! Christina, darling *(hugging her)* Can you ever
forgive me? I was mad to doubt you, but I was so jealous. I
wanted you so.

CHRIS. *(amazed and happy)* Then you don't think it was
immodest and shameless, to take Godiva's place?

EDGAR. It was glorious!

CHRIS. But I don't understand. Uncle Steven said . . . .

EDGAR. To hell with Uncle Steven! He told me a lot of high-
faluting rubbish about *you,* too. Woman, how dare you act
so chaste and timid and virginal? You've been driving me out
of my mind!

CHRIS. And how dare you act so cold and austere and
unemotional? I was at my wits' end.

EDGAR. *(holding her close)* I'll never believe a bishop again.

Oh, darling, I've been so miserable.

CHRIS. So have I, but it's all over now and I'm so happy I could burst.

EDGAR. *(still embracing her but looking beyond her at* LEO *who sits dumbly looking at nothing)* Christina, my love, I think we ought to go away from here. It's not fair to be so happy in front of others who are sad.

CHRIS. *(breaking from him in remorse)* Godiva! Oh, poor Godiva! Poor Leo! Whatever can we do?

EDGAR. I don't really think there's much we *can* do. Words of comfort are so pointless in a case like this. Perhaps the kindest thing would be to leave them alone.

CHRIS. No, that's not good enough. I can't have our happiness created out of their distress. I know! I'll fetch Mother! *She'll* know what to do. *(She runs out at the back)*

EDGAR. I hope so. *(There is an awkward pause.* THOMAS *coughs nervously)* Thomas, this is a personal affair. I think you ought to go.

THOMAS. *(coming forward)* Well, my lord, I . . . .

EDGAR. But before you go I must thank you very much for what you did just now. It required great courage. My wife and I are very much indebted to you. Here, this isn't much by way of a reward, but. . . . .*(He goes to open his purse, but* THOMAS *stops him)*

THOMAS. No, my lord, please. I'd rather not.

EDGAR. You're right, Thomas. Money can't buy honesty like yours.

THOMAS. And money won't be much use where *I'm* going.

EDGAR. Where you're going? Prison, you mean? *(in sudden anger)* Man, if they send you to prison I'll tell the whole world the shameful story. Do you hear, Leo? Godiva? This man shall not go to prison for what he did.

*(LEO merely shakes his head a little. GODIVA looks up with
tearful hatred.)*

GODIVA. Let him get out of my sight! Let him get out of my
sight!

THOMAS. Well, that's a reasonable request. I didn't keep my
job long, did I? Back to the bakery, I suppose. *(starts towards
exit, left)*

EDGAR. Thomas, if you're out of a job, how would you like to
come and join my household? I couldn't pay as much as
Leofric, but if you were a good servant you'd get your reward.

THOMAS. *(eagerly)* Indeed, I'd like nothing better sir. It's a pity
to leave the earl but, well . . . .he wouldn't want anyone
hanging around who knew the truth, would he?

EDGAR. That's very true.

THOMAS. Oh sir, there's Margery, the serving girl. She knows
too, I believe.

EDGAR. Then she must come to Lichfield too. Christina needs
another maid. Godiva, is that all right? Shall we take Margery
too?

GODIVA. Yes, take her. I never want to set eyes on her again.
*(EDGAR and THOMAS move to the left. GODIVA gets up
and goes to LEO)* Leo, I know I've let you down, but can't
you try to understand? I was so frightened. So terribly
frightened. Leo, please forgive me. Say you forgive me, Leo,
please!
*(She clutches his arm. He pushes her off, rises and turns away,
up centre. He sees HILDA enter and pause in the back
archway with eyes flashing, so he turns away, right, goes to
window, leans elbows on window sill and covers ears with
hands. He does not hear a word of the next scene. GODIVA
sits on step, right of centre, with head bowed on arms and
pays no attention to the next scene. OLD MOLL is still*

huddled on bench, down left.)
HILDA. So!
EDGAR. *(moving forward)* Mother, has Christina told you . . . .?
HILDA. Christina has explained everything.
EDGAR. Then you know why . . . .
HILDA. I know why Godiva is weeping and why Leo is sulking. I
    also know why Christina is in a state of rapture and why you,
    Edgar, are fairly on tenterhooks to get out of here and go to
    her.
EDGAR. Well, it's just that I . . . I want her to go and get a
    splinter out of my hand.
HILDA. *(gravely)* Indeed? That is a matter of some urgency,
    my son. You had better go to her at once.
    *(EDGAR rushes out at back, rushes back in and gives HILDA
    a smacking kiss on the cheek and rushes out again. HILDA
    lifts her eyebrows and adjusts her headdress with a smile)*
HILDA. *(stern again)* And now . . . .where is the wretch who is
    responsible for this unhappy state of affairs?
THOMAS. My lady, I could do no other. It was a case of . . .
HILDA. *(stopping him with a gesture)* Not you, young man. You
    did your best to set things right. No, I mean the old witch
    who cooked up this unholy dish out of sheer wanton mischief.
    Old Moll, I can see you, hiding your ugly face behind your
    fine new garments.
MOLL. *(rising as HILDA bears down on her)* If it's ugly faces
    we're discussing . . . . .
HILDA. It's not. It's ugly thoughts masquerading as magical
    visions and ugly hearts planning the downfall of simple
    trusting souls.
MOLL. You'd best beware how you speak to Old Moll or you
    may rue the day . . .
HILDA. The only one who'll do any rueing is you. Look at that

unhappy man over there! *(points to* LEO*)* What harm has he done to you? He has shown you kindliness and trust bordering on insanity, and how do you repay him? By exposing his wife as a liar, a coward and an imposter!

MOLL. But I never knew she was all that!

HILDA. You never knew! You set her a task that required daring and courage beyond her powers, you saw what a state of terror she was in at the very thought of it . . . . and you never guessed that she would fail? You never guessed that someone else took her place?

MOLL. No. Did you?

HILDA. Yes, of course I did. I know my daughter's limitations.

MOLL. And you never told?

HILDA. Why should I? Things were very nice as they were. Godiva had found a new importance and Leo could look forward to a place in history. Now, thanks to your meddling, all that is ruined, you stupid old faggot!

MOLL. *(cringing)* Well, I'm ever so sorry.

HILDA. Sorry! It's no use being sorry. You've got to do something to put things right.

MOLL. What can a poor old woman like me . . . . . ?

HILDA. Poor old woman, my foot! *(She gives a quick glance at* LEO, *who still has his hands over his ears, and at* GODIVA, *who is crushed and unheeding. She speaks with venomous quietness)* What do you usually do when you want a bit of excitement? You have a vision!

MOLL. Oh, but my visions . . . .

HILDA. Well, you'd better have another vision now, you old charlatan, and make it a good one.

MOLL. I can't!

HILDA. Why not?

MOLL. I can't just make it happen.

HILDA. You're going to this time. *(She takes out knife from sheath hanging at her belt)*

MOLL. But I only get visions on an empty stomach!

HILDA. *(gripping her)* I'll empty it for you!

MOLL. You wouldn't dare.

HILDA. You think not? I slashed those pictures, remember? And what's more I enjoyed it. Now . . . . *(still quiet, but very fierce)* are you going to have a vision?

MOLL. What sort of a vision?

HILDA. A vision of hope and promise. A vision of the future. The best you've ever had.

MOLL. But I can't think of anything. I have to be inspired.

HILDA. I'll inspire you! *(She swings her round so that she is between HILDA and LEO)* Now start. And make it good! *(She swings the knife and gives MOLL a vicious jab in the buttocks. MOLL lets out a piercing scream and wildly claps hands to the affected area. GODIVA looks up. LEO swings round, startled out of his silence.)*

LEO. Moll! Are you mad?

HILDA. *(still gripping her arm, unseen by LEO and GODIVA)* Hush Leo, I think she's going to have a vision.

LEO. A vision? I thought she was being murdered.

HILDA. They often scream when the magic spirit enters into them. Having a vision is quite a painful business, I believe.

MOLL. *(groaning and swaying and looking round in a hunted way)* Oooooooh! Ooooooh!

HILDA. *(still gripping her)* Poor thing, how she suffers. I think this will be a remarkable experience for all of us.

GODIVA. How she rolls her eyes! I wonder what she can see?

LEO. She doesn't see *us* any more. She's in another world.

HILDA. Yes. Or if she isn't she soon will be. *(She gives MOLL a smaller jab on the side hidden from the others. MOLL leaps *again and gives another cry)* There now, the spirits are crying out from within her. Tell us, Moll. Tell us what you can see. *(Writhing, MOLL sinks to the ground, face in hands. After a moment she starts to mutter and at first it is hard to hear what she says.)*

MOLL. Godiva. Godiva. The name goes on and on, year after year. Godiva of Coventry. *(louder)* Godiva of Coventry. The children read about her. They learn with reverence of what she did. Who rode the white horse, children? Who saved the people from Leofric's cruelty? Godiva. Godiva, nobody else. The years go by, hundreds of years. The story lives on. Good deeds and charities are done in her name. Holidays, carnivals, processions, all built on the legend of Godiva. Who rode the white horse, children? Who saved the people from Leofric's cruelty? Never forget Godiva . . . . .

(A change comes over her face. She begins to look frightened. She is silent but her eyes look up in wonder.)

GODIVA. I *shall* be famous, in spite of everything.

LEO. Hush, dear. She hasn't finished.

MOLL. What can I see? What can I hear? It's night time and there's a heavy droning in my ears. Then all around me is loud thunder and sudden bright flashes. Something is on fire! The fire is so big and hot! What can be burning? Is it Coventry that's burning? Oh, heaven help us all, Coventry is burning! *(She gets to her feet)*

GODIVA. Leo, I'm frightened. *(LEO goes and puts his arm round her)*

MOLL. *(more quietly)* Nothing is left but a mass of charred ruins. Coventry is in ruins. But the people set to work and build a new city. Strange new buildings, a new Coventry, very strange and very different. It frightens my old eyes. I don't think I like it. There's nothing familiar here. I'm in a strange land.

Nothing is left of the old days. *(Her anxious face softens)* Yes, there *is* something. I was wrong. Something familiar stands in the middle of these strange new buildings. It's a statue; life size and very beautiful. It's a lady on a white horse! It's Godiva, still young and beautiful after all these hundreds of years! Never forgotten. Right in the heart of Coventry. Never forgotten.

(Her voice dies away. After a pause she gives a deep sigh and turns to HILDA.*)*

Are you satisfied?

HILDA. *(looking at her in wonder)* Yes. You've done well.

MOLL. I think I'll go and have a sit down in the kitchen.

HILDA. Yes, do. And Moll, you can keep that dress you're wearing. I'll explain to my daughter. *(*MOLL *nods and exits, left.)*

LEO. What a remarkable old woman! I never heard anything like it.

GODIVA. Do you think it's true? That I'll never be forgotten and that there'll be a life size statue of me in the middle of Coventry hundreds of years from now?

LEO. I can't help but believe it. Old Moll was in the grip of some magic power. She's a true visionary, I reckon.

GODIVA. I believed her too. Did you, mother?

HILDA. Strangely enough, yes. I believed her too.

GODIVA. Leo darling, does it make a difference? Please say it does and be kind to me again. I can't bear it if you turn your back on me.

LEO. After this vision of Moll's I don't feel angry any more. Of course I'll be kind to you dear. You couldn't help what happened, and to tell you the truth I didn't like being married to that proud and overbearing beauty that's been the centre of attraction all day.

GODIVA. You mean you'd rather have that silly, frightened creature that I used to be?

LEO. Well, of course I would. It made me feel clever and strong and superior. I always knew I'd married the ideal wife. *(He puts his arm round her to lead her off stage)*

GODIVA. Oh, Leo, I think you're wonderful!
(They go out, smiling at each other.)

HILDA. *(watching them go)* Wonderful? She thinks he's wonderful! Perhaps she's right.
(Enter MARGERY, down left.)

MARGERY. May I come and prepare the table, madam?

HILDA. *(Coming down to centre front)* Yes, of course, Margery. *(MARGERY goes out, left. THOMAS at last ventures forth from behind bench where he has been keeping very still and quiet.)*

HILDA. Well, Thomas, I hope there'll be no more talk of prison for you.

THOMAS. No, Lady Hilda, I'm to come to Lichfield and serve your other daughter and her husband.

HILDA. Splendid. I hope you'll be happy there.

THOMAS. I know I will. I'm devoted to Lady Christina.

HILDA. Mm. Yes, that reminds me. My daughter Christina asked me to tell you something.

THOMAS. *(eagerly)* A message? For me?

HILDA. *(troubled)* Yes. I hardly know how to say it.
(Enter MARGERY with tray laden with platters, tankards, bread, fruit etc.)

THOMAS. Have I annoyed her in some way?

HILDA. Oh no. On the contrary. She's overwhelmed with gratitude for what you did. It was the act of a very brave man and a hero. *(MARGERY looks at THOMAS with new respect)*

THOMAS. I could hardly stand by and let her husband suspect

her of . . . . . of *that*.

HILDA. No, of course not. Husbands are such suspicious
    creatures, aren't they? It wouldn't have been any use telling
    him that Cedric is like an elder brother to her. He'd never have
    believed that Christina could have passed a whole hour, just
    talking to him . . . . . would he? With the door bolted, too?
    No-one would consider that very likely, would they, even
    though Cedric is the greatest gossip on earth.

THOMAS. *(puzzled)* No, my lady.

HILDA. Would *you* believe it? That they were only talking?

THOMAS. If Lady Christina said so. I'd believe her of course.
    She's incapable of unfaithfulness, as that old fool Moll should
    have guessed. But since she wasn't with Cedric anyway, the
    question doesn't arise. Old Moll's lying mouth was properly
    stopped this time.

HILDA. Old Moll makes mistakes sometimes, but I've never
    known her tell a lie, Thomas.

THOMAS. Beg pardon, my lady, but you weren't there when she
    said it. A nastier, more spiteful and deliberate lie I never did
    hear. And I've heard some lies in my time.

HILDA. So have I, Thomas. Some lies are spiteful, it's true . . . .
    but some are gallant, like the one *you* told.

THOMAS. Me, my lady? I told no lie!

HILDA. Well, I wasn't there to hear it, of course, but Christina
    asked me to say this . . . "A man who could lie as gallantly as
    you did deserves a better reward than I can give".

THOMAS. *(amazed)* She told you that?

HILDA. *(moving up towards exit at back)* She did. Those were
    her very words. And then she tacked on an afterthought. *(She
    stands in archway. looking at him kindly)* She said, "Tell
    Thomas that Margery's hair is as black as mine".
    (Exit HILDA *at back.)*

THOMAS. *(not yet understanding)* I don't get it. "A man who could lie as gallantly as . . . . " but I didn't.

MARGERY. *(Who has finished laying the table)* Didn't you?

THOMAS. And what did she mean about your hair?

MARGERY. *(picking up tray and coming down centre)* It's as black as hers.

THOMAS. Well, what of it? Dozens of girls have . . . . . . Oh!

(Realization dawns. There is a long pause while shock, dismay, wonder and finally admiration show in his face. MARGERY watches him with a shy smile.)

THOMAS. *(going towards her)* Margery! Your hair is as black as hers!

MARGERY. *(shyly and rather proudly)* Yes. And what's more, it's three inches longer!

(They are standing gazing at each other with the tray between them when she is overcome by an attack of sneezing. She thrusts the tray into his hands, turns her head away and continues sneezing and laughing until the curtain falls.)

CURTAIN.

PROPERTY PLOT.

ACT ONE.

Set:- Tapestries on walls. *(These could be painted on to scenery)* Up right, refectory table with pitcher, two cups and bowl and apples on it. One cup contains wine.
In front of this is a bench, and there is another bench down left. Two carved wooden chairs with arms, one centre, one down right. Woven rush mat on floor.
For Margery - a besom for sweeping floor.

ACT TWO. On table - cold meat, bread, ale, 4 metal plates and four tankards.
For Margery - large wooden tray.
Cloth to wipe table.

ACT THREE. For Edgar - large needle:
purse with money, attached to belt.
For Hilda - Knife in sheath attached to belt.
For Margery - tray laden with platters, tankards and bread.

REHEARSAL DATES

CAST NOTES